The Differences of the Imams

In the name of Allah, Most Gracious Most Merciful.
All praise be to Allah, Lord of the Worlds, and peace and blessings be upon His Messenger Muḥammad, Mercy to the Worlds.

THE DIFFERENCES OF THE IMAMS

Shaykh al-Ḥadīth
Mawlānā Muḥammad Zakariyyā Kāndhlawī

Translated by
Mawlānā Muhammad Kadwa

WHITE THREAD PRESS
SANTA BARBARA • CALIFORNIA • USA

First U.S. Edition September 2004

ISBN 0-9728358-2-2

Published by:
White Thread Press
California USA
www.whitethreadpress.com
info@whitethreadpress.com

Distributed in the UK by Azhar Academy Ltd. London
sales@azharacademy.com
Tel: +44 (208) 534 9191

Library of Congress Cataloging-in-Publication Data

Muḥammad Zakariyyā, 1898–
[Ikhtilāf al-a'immah. English]
The Differences of the Imams / Shaykh al-Hadith Mawlana Muhammad Zakariyya Kandhlawi; translated by Mawlana Muhammad Kadwa; edited by White Thread Press.–1st US ed.
p. cm.
Includes bibliographical references and index.
ISBN 0-9728358-2-2 (pbk. : alk. paper)
1. Hadith Criticism, Interpretation, etc. 2. Sunna. 3. Islamic Law–Interpretation and Construction. 4. Islamic law–Sources. I. Title.
KBP450.M8413 2004
340.5'9–dc22
2004008321

Printed and bound in the United States of America on acid-free paper

If a contingent from every expedition go forth to devote themselves to studies in religion, and admonish the people when they return to them—that they (may learn) to guard themselves (against evil).

—The Qur'ān 9:122

TRANSLITERATION KEY

ء (أ إ) ’ (A slight catch in the breath. It is also used to indicate where the *hamza* has been dropped from the beginning of a word.

ا a, ā

ب b

ت t

ث th (Should be pronounced as the *th* in *thin* or *thirst*).

ج j

ح ḥ (Tensely breathed *h* sound).

خ kh (Pronounced like the *ch* in Scottish *loch* with the mouth hollowed to produce a full sound).

د d

ذ dh (Should be pronounced as the *th* in *this* or *that*).

ر r

ز z

س s

ش sh

ص ṣ (A heavy *s* pronounced far back in the mouth with the mouth hollowed to produce a full sound).

ض ḍ (A heavy *d/dh* pronounced far back in the mouth with the mouth hollowed to produce a full sound).

ط ṭ (A heavy *t* pronounced far back in the mouth with the mouth hollowed to produce a full sound).

ظ ẓ (A heavy *dh* pronounced far back in the mouth with the mouth hollowed to produce a full sound).

ع ʿ, ʿa, ʿi, ʿu (Pronounced from the throat).

غ gh (Pronounced like a throaty French *r* with the mouth hollowed to produce a full sound).

ف f

ق q (A guttural *q* sound with the mouth hollowed to produce a full sound).

ك k

ل l

م m

ن n

و w, u, u.

ه h

ي y, ī, i

ﷻ Used following the mention of Allah, translated as, “His majesty is exalted.”

ﷺ Used following the mention of the Messenger Muḥammad, translated as, “May Allah bless him and give him peace.”

رضي الله عنه Used following the mention of a Companion of the Messenger, translated as, “May Allah be pleased with him.”

رضي الله عنهم Used following the mention of more than one Companion of the Messenger (and also after a female Companion in this work for lack of an appropriate glyph), translated as, “May Allah be pleased with them.”

Publisher's Note

The Differences of the Imams, a translation of *Ikhtilāf al-a'imma* by Shaykh al-Ḥadīth Mawlānā Muḥammad Zakariyyā Kāndhlawī, was originally published in Shaʿbān 1418/December 1997 by Madrasah Arabia Islamia, Azaadville, South Africa, and was subsequently published in the UK in 1999. The author's popularity and his limpid writing style, coupled with the lucid English translation by Mawlānā Muhammad Kadwa and the then heightened interest in the work's subject matter, together contributed to the tremendous acceptance that the book received.

White Thread Press now presents an edited and revised edition of Mawlānā Muhammad Kadwa's translation, published for the first time in the US, with kind permission from Madrasah Arabia Islamia, Azaadville. White Thread Press has made every effort to produce this edition with total fidelity to the original work and the translation, but some refinements were deemed necessary. They are as follows.

The translation has been reviewed alongside portions of the original Urdu text to assure complete accuracy, and its language has been thoroughly edited for increased clarity. Chapter titles and subsections have been more clearly defined and other relevant headings added where deemed necessary. Part 2, section 3 has been rearranged for clarity. Any additions to the text made by the original translator or by the editors have been placed in parentheses. The style and format of the book have been modified to conform to the standards of

White Thread Press. A more standardized transliteration of Arabic terms has been adopted, with appropriate diacritical marks for more precise transliteration. A transliteration key has also been included to allow the reader easier reference to the original Arabic terminology. The glossary has been updated, and an index has been added. Finally, a more detailed biography of the author has been appended at the end of the book to give insight into his caliber as a scholar of the Islamic sciences in general, and in particular as a master of the science of ḥadīth, a subject to which he devoted over sixty years of his life, until his death in Madīna, the Illuminated City of the Prophet Muḥammad ﷺ.

May Allah ﷻ accept this work that White Thread Press offers to the English-speaking world, and may He bless all who have assisted in preparing it and overlook any mistakes and shortcomings they may have made in doing so.

Contents

Part Two
The Era of The Companions & Followers ﷺ

Part Three
The Era of The Mujtahid Imams & Some Principles of Ḥadīth and Jurisprudence

Author's Foreword

We praise Allah ﷻ and send blessings upon His noble Messenger ﷺ, and upon His Messenger's family, his Companions, his followers, and the upholders of the true faith.

To proceed. In Ramadan 1346 AH, a monthly digest entitled *"Al-Maẓāhir"* was launched by Madrasa Maẓāhir ʿUlūm (Saharanpur) under the editorship of my dear friend respected Mawlānā Jalīl, who at that time was a teacher at the above-mentioned institute and is presently the Muftī of Jāmiʿa Ashrafiyya, Lahore. At the insistence of Mawlānā Jalīl, I started writing articles for this monthly digest on the topic of "The Differences of the Imams" [*Ikhtilāf al-a'imma*], inspite of my inefficiency and incapability. Despite the barrage of engagements, I continued writing a few pages each month for this magazine. However, due to certain circumstances, the said magazine terminated publication after about fourteen months. Consequently, my humble articles also came to an end. Many friends and editors of other magazines strongly insisted I complete this series but to no avail. I was able to write for the first magazine simply because the editor Mawlānā Jalīl was a teacher at the *madrasa* and he was always around to ask me to write. However, at the termination of this magazine, inspite of my own desire and the insistence of my colleagues, the book could not reach completion.

My initial intention was to compile a detailed and comprehensive book on this subject but my various academic [*ʿilmī*] as well as literary [*ta'līfī*] engagements precluded the realization of this intention. At that time, some friends insisted I publish whatever had been completed as part one of this book. Since (I felt) the subject matter was deficient, I had planned to publish it once some more (material) was added to it. However, now there remains no hope whatsoever of fulfilling this ambition. Excessive ailments have rendered me totally helpless and here I am sitting on the edge of the grave.

Mawlānā Muḥammad Shāhid and other sincere friends insisted that whatever had been compiled is not devoid of benefit. So, (following my permission), Mawlānā Muḥammad Shāhid decided to print whatever has been compiled.

May Allah Most High grant blessing [*baraka*] in this, may He benefit the people from it, and may He bless Mawlānā Shāhid with success in this world as well as the next. *Āmīn*.

My success is only from Allah, upon Him do I place my trust, and to Him do I turn.

Introduction

All praise is due to Allah ﷻ and peace and salutations upon the Messenger Muḥammad ﷺ.

For some time now people have been occupied with the question that, since the Imams (of various schools) have established everything from the sayings and practices of the Messenger of Allah ﷺ, why are there differences of opinion among them? The numerous sessions of debates and the excessive number of publications on the issues of controversy have rendered the problem even more menacing. The issue has reached such dire proportions that those who object (to why the Imams have differed) have split into two groups. The first group is hopelessly trapped in their evil thoughts of the Imams, so much so that even if they wish to disentangle themselves from this vicious web just out of good thought for the Imams, they are unable to free themselves from this trap because they are further ensnared by the apparent disparity between the sayings of the Imams and some of the clear source texts.

The second group, on the other hand, has gone even further and, let alone the Imams, they have started harboring insolent thoughts about the Messenger of Allah ﷺ himself, simply because of the apparently contradictory ḥadīths transmitted from him. However, the fault lies in referring to (English or) Urdu translations of the ḥadīths, because in order to get a clear picture of the meaning, one has to posses the intellectual capacity to comprehend the ḥadīths together with a proper understanding of the background and the prelude of the ḥadīths. In the absence of these prerequisites, the mere translation of the ḥadīths is bound to lead to objections and misgivings.

The repercussions of these differences have reached such proportions that people have split up into various sects grappling and contending with one another. The *wuḍū'* of one group is considered invalid by the other, while the *ṣalāt* of one group is considered void by the other, and so forth. In *zakāt, ṣawm, ḥajj,* and virtually every other act of worship [*ʿibāda*] as well, there is inevitably some difference or other which has led to people debating with one another.

Therefore, it has become necessary to expose the basis of the differences (of opinion) found among the Imams. The reasons for these differences, dating back to the first epoch of Islam, will be expounded upon to demonstrate that the apparently contradictory texts of the ḥadīths leave no scope for doubting the Messenger of Allah ﷺ, nor do they give anyone the right to cast aspersions on the Companions [*ṣaḥāba*] ﷺ, the Followers [*tābiʿīn*] or the Imams (may Allah ﷻ have mercy on them all). The fact is that all the Imams [*mujtahidīn*] were leaders of the correct path and they encouraged and guided the masses toward the correct path as well. Any slanderous remark cast against them is a sure sign of the deprivation of Allah's mercy [*ḥirmān*]. May Allah ﷻ protect us. *Āmīn.*

There is obviously no doubt about the importance of this issue. I would have preferred to see the topic addressed by someone much more capable than myself. I pray that my writing does not merely add to the confusion rather than clarifying the matter.

Nevertheless, I had excused myself from this mammoth task, but the insistence of the people of Maẓāhir ʿUlūm compelled me to put pen to paper. While acknowledging my incompetence, I present my disordered work.

The differences among the Imams are divided into three stages. The first involves contradictory narrations [*riwāyāt*]; in other words, the apparent contradictions between the words and deeds of Allah's

Messenger ﷺ. The second stage deals with the contradictions found in the *āthār*, meaning the apparent contradictions between the words and actions of the Companions [*ṣaḥāba*] and Followers [*tābiʿīn*]. The third stage encompasses the differences found among the schools of thought [*madhāhib*]; in other words, the apparent contradictions between the recognized opinions of the various Imams, which later became the established views of their followers.

Since these differences have occurred at three stages, I consider it necessary to write briefly on each of these stages. Also, since the second and third stages of these differences are actually an offshoot of the first stage, I will base my writings according to the same order as well. And from Allah ﷻ do we seek divine guidance.

Part One

The Era of the Messenger

The Primary Reason
Varying Commands for Different People and Circumstances

During the time of the Messenger of Allah ﷺ, the present-day system of imparting Islamic law was not in operation. There were no comprehensive books of Islamic jurisprudence [*fiqh*] available and no in-depth compilations on specialized subjects. The fundamentals, etiquette, conditions and interdictions of the laws [*aḥkām*] and rulings [*masā'il*] were not recorded separately. The only method of imparting Islamic rulings was that whenever a command was revealed, the Messenger of Allah ﷺ used to inform the people verbally and demonstrate it practically. Once the verses of *wuḍū'* [ablution] were revealed, he ﷺ showed his community how to perform *wuḍū'*. When the verses of *ṣalāt* were revealed, the Angel Jibra'īl ﵇ actually demonstrated the correct procedure of *ṣalāt* before the Messenger of Allah ﷺ, and he in turn taught the *Umma* how to perform *ṣalāt*. There were no distinctions whatsoever between a certain act being *farḍ* or *wājib*, or a certain posture being a *sunna* or integral [*rukn*], etc. The Messenger's ﷺ demonstration left no complexities or uncertainties.

Even the Companions ﵃ refrained from digressing into possibilities and rationalities. If someone had to finely examine or challenge these laws, it was considered rude and such a person would be admonished for his impudence.

ʿAbdullāh ibn ʿUmar ﵄ once narrated that Allah's Messenger ﷺ said, "A person should not prevent his wife attending the *masjid* if she wishes to perform *ṣalāt* therein." One of Ibn ʿUmar's sons, considering the prevalent conditions (of his time), declared "We will not allow them to attend *ṣalāt* at the *masjid*." Since this statement was in apparent contrast to the ḥadīth of Allah's Messenger ﷺ, Ibn ʿUmar ؓ found it extremely offensive and not only did he admonish his son, but according to the narration of *Musnad Aḥmad*, he refrained from speaking to him right until his death.

Similarly, Ibn ʿUmar ؓ was once asked if *witr ṣalāt* was *wājib* or *sunna*. He responded: "The Messenger of Allah ﷺ as well as the Companions [*ṣaḥāba*] ؓ always performed the *witr ṣalāt.*" The questioner continued asking the same question repeatedly and Ibn ʿUmar ؓ continued to provide the same answer.

The reason for his unwavering answer was simply to draw attention to the fact that those who sincerely wish to practice Islam will not delve into any intricacies. If Allah's Messenger ﷺ and his Companions ؓ consistently carried out a certain action, its obligation [*wujūb*] is self-evident. In short, the laws of Islam used to be taught in a practical manner according to the need of the occasion. The Companions ؓ used to detest questions based on mere assumption: questions such as, "If a certain act is omitted in *wuḍū'* or something additional is done, what is the ruling?"

Ibn ʿUmar ؓ says that ʿUmar ؓ invoked the curse of Allah ﷻ on a person who posed hypothetical questions. The Companions ؓ would only ask the Messenger of Allah ﷺ about issues [*masā'il*] which occurred in reality. Allah's Messenger ﷺ would then issue a verdict according to the circumstances and conditions of the questioner. Differences and contradictory narrations are quite obviously destined to follow from this. A few examples are listed below which demonstrate this fact even more explicitly.

Imam Muslim narrates on the authority of ʿAbdullāh ibn ʿUmar ؓ that a blind Companion [*ṣaḥābī*] once approached Allah's Messenger ﷺ and submitted: "I did not have anyone to guide me to the *masjid*, please excuse my absence from the *masjid* for the congregational *ṣalāt* and permit me to perform my *ṣalāt* at home." The Messenger of Allah ﷺ granted him permission. However, when he learnt that this Companion lived in close proximity to the *masjid* and he was able to hear the *adhān,* the Messenger ﷺ withdrew his permission and ordered the man to join the congregational *ṣalāt* in the *masjid.* Conversely, in the case of ʿItbān ibn Mālik ؓ, Allah's Messenger ﷺ accepted his excuse of blindness and exempted him from attending the congregational *ṣalāt.*

Allah's Messenger ﷺ had permitted ʿAbdullāh ibn Zayd ؓ, who had heard the words of the call to prayer [*adhān*] in a dream to make the call to commence [*iqāma*] inspite of Bilāl ؓ calling out the *adhān.* However, once on a journey, Ziyad ibn Ḥārith al-Ṣudāʾī ؓ called out the *adhān* and Bilāl ؓ was about to call out the *iqāma* when the Messenger of Allah ﷺ said, "Whosoever calls out the *adhān*, has the right to call out the *iqāma* as well." Saying this, he restrained Bilāl from calling out the *iqāma.*

Once, Abū Bakr ؓ gave his entire wealth in charity and Allah's Messenger ﷺ accepted it. However, when certain other Companions ؓ decided to give their entire wealth in charity, Allah's Messenger ﷺ did not accept it.

These are not isolated incidents. There are thousands of such incidents, which clearly demonstrate that the Messenger of Allah ﷺ issued varying orders for different people.

Abū Hurayra ؓ narrates that a person once asked Allah's Messenger ﷺ if he was permitted to hug and kiss his wife while fasting. The Messenger ﷺ granted him permission. However, when another Companion sought permission to do the same, he was declined permission. Abū Hurayra ؓ said, "I immediately understood the reason for the disparity between the two. The one who was permitted was an old man while the other Companion was a young man."

In cases like the above-mentioned incident, each narrator will narrate what he heard directly from Allah's Messenger ﷺ. The person who was granted permission to kiss his wife while fasting will obviously narrate that hugging and kissing does not nullify the fast. However, the other person will narrate his ḥadīth in direct contrast to this and will vehemently deny the permissibility of kissing and hugging while fasting. This apparent contradiction between the two narrations is not only confined to two isolated narrators. In fact, there were always groups of students, devoted followers, enquirers, visitors, delegates, and others in the presence of Allah's Messenger ﷺ who would have heard these exchanges and related them according to their own understanding.

For this reason, the two groups who heard two conflicting laws would narrate only what they heard from Allah's Messenger ﷺ. Any number of conflicting narrations falling under this fundamental rule will still be considered negligible because every gathering consisted of various people, the exempted [*maʿdhūr*] as well as the healthy, the able-bodied as well as the weak. The law took into consideration the health of one and the weakness of the other. This is the reason for the apparent contradiction.

One of the people in the gathering was so strong-hearted that even if he gave all his wealth in charity, there was no fear of him ever complaining. Allah's Messenger ﷺ was quite confident that no matter what calamity afflicted that particular person, he would become ever more engrossed in turning his attention toward Allah ﷻ and totally at ease with the fate issued by Him.

On the other hand, there were other personalities in the gathering upon whom he did not have such confidence. In fact, there was a fear of them exceeding even the boundaries of lamentation if they gave away all of their wealth in charity. Hence, he prohibited them from doing so.

Similarly, for a traveler who is quite strong and able, it is most appropriate for him to fast in the holy month of Ramadan. He should not postpone the fasts when traveling, thereby forfeiting the great virtues of this month. On the other hand, if a person is extremely weak and fasting while traveling will most probably be detrimental to him, he is not permitted to fast. Due to such differences, the ḥadīths narrating laws pertinent to fasting while traveling are sure to differ as well.

Abū Saʿīd al-Khudrī ؓ narrates, "On the sixteenth of Ramadan we set out for a battle in the company of Allah's Messenger ﷺ. Some of our friends observed the fasts of Ramadan, while others decided not to fast. However, each group had no objection against the other. Those fasting did not accuse those abstaining nor did the latter challenge the former."

Hamza ibn ʿAmr Aslamī ؓ narrates that he once asked the Messenger of Allah ﷺ whether, since he was in a habit of fasting excessively, it would be permissible for him to fast while traveling. Allah's Messenger ﷺ replied, "You are at liberty to fast or to abstain from fasting. You may do as you please." However, Jābir ؓ narrates that Allah's Messenger ﷺ said, "There is no good in fasting while traveling." In fact, one ḥadīth even refers to those who fast when traveling as sinners. Notwithstanding this, ʿAbd al-Raḥmān ibn ʿAwf ؓ narrates that Allah's Messenger ﷺ said, "The one who fasts while traveling is like a person who breaks his fast while at home."

In short, the disparity of narrations stems from the disparity of conditions. As evident from the aforementioned incidents, the Messenger of Allah ﷺ (sometimes) issued two utterly different orders for different individuals. The group that was present when the first order was given will obviously differ from the group that was present when the second order was issued. As a result, two large groups became narrators of two totally conflicting rulings.

There could have been, in fact there were, some people who were present in both gatherings, and they were most certainly compelled to ponder over the disparity between the rulings and reach a decision whereby both rulings are taken into account. As explained above, Abū Hurayra ؓ provided the conflicting narrations about kissing and hugging while fasting. He narrated the reason for the disparity as well.

There are thousands of other similar incidents, which cannot be contained here wholly, and it is not our purpose to do so here. Even though the aforementioned fact (regarding the difference of narrations) is quite evident, a few testimonial incidents proving this fact were provided merely to drive the point home.

Following such diverging narrations, the responsibility now falls upon the Companions [*ṣaḥāba*], the Followers [*tābiʿīn*], and the *mujtahid* Imams to determine the source, occasion and correct juncture of each narration, and they should interpret each narration according to the demands of the occasion.

Reason 2
A Special Case is Taken as a General Order

The second reason for contradictory narrations is that at times, the Messenger of Allah ﷺ issued an exclusive order for a particular person due to some special reason, and the audience [*majlis*] was led to believe that it was a general order and not a restricted order. Thus, they started narrating it as a general rule.

For example, according to ʿĀ'isha ﷺ, Ibn ʿUmar ﷺ narrates that Allah's Messenger ﷺ said, "The deceased is punished due to the crying of his house folk."

ʿĀ'isha ﷺ rejected this interpretation. According to her, Allah's Messenger ﷺ made this statement in regard to a Jewish woman whose household was crying over her.

Apparent Contradictions in the Ḥadīths

Allow me to point out at this juncture that we do not wish to elaborate on the category of this ḥadīth, nor do we wish to comment on it, nor do we wish to ascertain whether ʿĀ'isha's ﷺ ḥadīth or Ibn ʿUmar's ﷺ ḥadīth is given preference. All we wish to clarify here is that such degrees of disparity and contradiction exist in the field of ḥadīth study.

For example, according to the Ḥanafī school of thought, the *ṣalāt* for greeting the *masjid* [*taḥiyyat al-masjid*] is prohibited while the Friday sermon [*khuṭba*] is in progress. However, one ḥadīth makes mention of a very poor Companion named Sulayk al-Ghaṭafānī ﷺ who entered the *masjid* while the *khuṭba* was in progress. Allah's Messenger ﷺ ordered the Companion to perform *taḥiyyat al-masjid* so that the people could witness his poverty and constrained circumstances. Together with this, they also witnessed this special concession awarded to this particular Companion in that Allah's Messenger ﷺ ordered him to perform supererogatory [*nafl*] *ṣalāt* while the sermon was in progress. According to certain narrations, Allah's Messenger ﷺ brought the sermon to a halt and remained standing to enable this Companion to complete his *ṣalāt*.

On the basis of this narration, many people considered this action as a general ruling, and as an all-encompassing principle they narrate that a person who enters the *masjid* while the Friday sermon is in progress should perform two *rakʿāts* [units] of *taḥiyyat al-masjid*.

The story of suckling Sālim, the slave of Abū Hudhayfa ﷺ is also of a similar nature. ʿĀ'isha ﷺ narrates that Sahla bint Suhayl ﷺ came to Allah's Messenger ﷺ and submitted, "O Messenger of Allah, I perceive a feeling of displeasure on (my husband) Abū Hudhayfa's face whenever Sālim, our freed slave, comes before me." Allah's Messenger ﷺ advised: "Breastfeed him." She replied, "He is a bearded adult." He said, "Go ahead and breastfeed him. You will not perceive any displeasure on Abū Hudhayfa's face thereafter."

On the basis of this narration, ʿĀ'isha ﷺ considered this a general rule while the other wives of Allah's Messenger ﷺ rejected this opinion. Umm Salama ﷺ, the wife of Allah's Messenger ﷺ, comments on this: "We are not aware of the actual reason for this command. However, we are confident that this rule was specifically confined to Sālim only."

Ibn Qutayba narrates in his book *Ta'wīl mukhtalaf al-ḥadīth* that ʿImrān ibn Ḥusayn ﷺ says, "By Allah, I know so many ḥadīths that I can narrate rather extensively if I want to, but the practice of certain Companions ﷺ impede me from doing so. They (i.e. those Companions) heard many ḥadīths from Allah's Messenger ﷺ like I did, and they remained in his service like I did, but some of them have committed many inaccuracies while narrating. I fear that if I had to narrate, then the narration of the ḥadīths would bewilder me just as they were left bewildered. However, let me draw your attention to the fact that this was only an oversight on their part and they had no intention of committing these blunders."

It was for the same reason that ʿUmar ﷺ prohibited the people from excessive narration during his caliphate [*khilāfa*]. In fact, he even prevented some of the very senior Companions from excessive narrations of the ḥadīths.

Abū Salama ﷺ asked Abū Hurayra ﷺ if he used to narrate as abundantly during the time of ʿUmar ﷺ as he did in later times. Abū Hurayra ﷺ replied, "If I were narrating (then) like I am doing now, ʿUmar ﷺ would have cautioned me with his whip."

In short, the second reason for the apparent contradictions in the narrations is that at times, Allah's Messenger ﷺ issued a special command confined to one person only, but a narrator narrated it as a general rule. The examples have been explained above.

Reason 3
A General Order is Taken as a Special Case

The third reason for the apparent contradictions between narrations is the opposite of the second reason. In other words, Allah's Messenger ﷺ mentioned something as an all-encompassing rule, but the narrator confined it to specific individuals only.

One example is the narration of Ibn ʿUmar ﷺ regarding the punishment of the deceased. Ibn ʿUmar ﷺ narrated this as a general rule. However, ʿĀ'isha ﷺ said that this applied only to a particular incident of a Jewish woman who was being mourned by her family.

Hence, for the revision of such narrations, a great need is felt for the *mujtahids,* who are aware of all the various types of narrations. From these narrations, they are able to deduce which rules are of general application, which are special, and what the reasons are for rendering something permissible for one and impermissible for the other.

Reason 4
A Difference of Perception

Quite often, there are apparent contradictions in the narrations simply because various people saw Allah's Messenger ﷺ doing a certain thing and they all narrated it according to their own understanding of things. The beholders of any deed are obviously of diverse perception. Some of the witnesses were very discerning. They were able to understand every incident according to the occasion. On the other hand, some of them were not as discerning, but they had very retentive memories. They narrated certain events according to the way they understood them. Many examples of this can be found in the ḥadīths dealing with the pilgrimage [*ḥajj*]. For example, one of the narrators says that Allah's Messenger ﷺ made an *ifrād ḥajj* because he heard the Messenger ﷺ saying *"Labbayka bi ḥajjatin"* or "I have presented myself in Your service to perform the *ḥajj*." The narration itself is authentic and the narrator is not guilty of any deficiency. However, other people narrate that Allah's Messenger ﷺ performed a *qirān ḥajj*. This narration apparently seems contradictory to the first, because the *qirān ḥajj* is very different from the *ifrād ḥajj*. In actual fact though, there is no contradiction between the narrations, since it is permissible for one performing *qirān ḥajj* to also say *"Labbayka bi ḥajjatin"* (as Allah's Messenger ﷺ had uttered). Only a *mujtahid* is able to bring about some harmony between the apparently contradictory narrations and avoid undue confusion.

Similar is the ḥadīth dealing with the Messenger's ﷺ commencement of his *iḥrām* or "pilgrim sanctity." There are conflicting narrations as to exactly when Allah's Messenger ﷺ started his *iḥrām*. Due to this, the Imams have also differed as to when it is most virtuous for one to initiate one's *iḥrām*. Prompted by these very same contradictory narrations, Saʿīd ibn Jubayr, an outstanding Follower [*tābiʿī*], asked ʿAbdullāh ibn ʿAbbās to explain these contradictions. Imam Abū Dāwūd (may Allah ﷻ have mercy on him) transmits this narration in complete detail as follows:

> Saʿīd ibn Jubayr says, "I told ʿAbdullāh ibn ʿAbbās that I was extremely surprised with the contradictory narrations of the Companions regarding the commencement of the *iḥrām* [pilgrim sanctity] of Allah's Messenger ﷺ. I wondered why there were so many contradictory reports." ʿAbdullāh ibn ʿAbbās replied, "I am quite aware of the reason. Since Allah's Messenger ﷺ performed only one *ḥajj* after his migration to Madīna (and because it was toward the end of his life, a great number of people attended this *ḥajj*. The person who observed him doing a certain thing at a certain time regarded that as a principal element of *ḥajj*). This resulted in contradictory reports on his performance of *ḥajj*. The story of his *iḥrām* was also subjected to these contradictions. What happened was that en-route to Makka, Allah's Messenger ﷺ encamped at a place called Dhū al-Ḥulayfa. He performed two *rakʿats* of *ṣalāt* at the *masjid* and commenced his *iḥrām* at that point. Whoever witnessed this incident reported that he commenced his *iḥrām* in the *masjid* immediately after the two *rakʿats*.
>
> After this, Allah's Messenger ﷺ mounted his camel. The moment the camel started rising, Allah's Messenger ﷺ said "*labbayk*" once again, which was heard by a great number of people scattered around him. The people who heard him before knew that this was the second time he uttered "*labbayk*." However, those that heard this "*labbayk*" for the first time narrated that he started his *iḥrām* after he mounted the camel.
>
> Due to the large crowds of people, the Messenger of Allah's ﷺ voice could not reach all of them, nor could they all meet him at one time. Hence, they came to the Messenger ﷺ in small groups and asked him whatever they wished to know.

> Thereafter, the Messenger of Allah's ﷺ camel climbed the summit of Baydā and (since it is preferable for a pilgrim to say "*labbayk*" whenever he ascends a high point) he said "*labbayk*" loudly. The people who were around him at that time were under the impression that Allah's Messenger ﷺ commenced his *iḥrām* at Baydā. By Allah! Allah's Messenger ﷺ commenced his *iḥrām* at the spot he performed his two *rakʿats* of *iḥrām* prayer" (*Sunan Abī Dāwūd*).

Since Saʿīd ibn Jubayr heard various contradictory accounts of this *ḥajj*, he felt he should delve deeper into the true account of what exactly took place. ʿAbdullāh ibn ʿAbbās ﷺ was fully aware of what transpired, so he confidently explained exactly what happened. Since he was a jurist [*faqīh*] as well as a *mujtahid*, he also explained the reasons for the differences of narrations and at the same time he brought about harmony between all the narrations.

In contrast, if an ordinary layman is confronted with all these apparently contradictory narrations, the unfortunate person will be left perturbed and dumbfounded. Objections and various complications are thereafter bound to follow. At the end of it all, even the people who do not adhere to any *madhhab* [*ghayr muqallidīn*], in spite of their vehemence and prejudice, have no retreat but to make *taqlīd*, (i.e. resort to a school of thought [*madhhab*]).

In his book, *Sabīl al-Rashād*, Mawlānā (Rashīd Aḥmad) Gangōhī (may Allah be pleased with him) quotes an extract from the *Ishāʿat al-sunna* by Mawlānā Muḥammad Ḥusayn Batālwī, a leader of those who do not follow a traditional school in jurisprudence, who writes that a non-*mujtahid* has no retreat or option but to follow a *mujtahid* (*Ishāʿat al-sunna* 11:211). Mawlānā Batālwī further writes:

> After twenty-five years of experience, we have become aware of the fact that those who, out of ignorance, totally relinquish following a school altogether [*taqlīd*] eventually relinquish Islam altogether. Some of them convert to Christianity while some of them become atheists. The most *insignificant* outcome of this freedom is flagrant violation of Islamic law (*ibid* 11:53).

Reason 5
Intentional Action vs Coincidence

At times, many groups of people witnessed the Messenger of Allah ﷺ doing something. Some of them considered it coincidental and treated it as a natural and habitual activity of his. Others considered it intentional and willful, thereby narrating it as a *sunna* or *mustaḥab* [preferable] action. There are many examples of this nature in the books of ḥadīth. For example, on the occasion of the farewell pilgrimage, it is an accepted fact that the Messenger of Allah ﷺ camped at a place called Abṭaḥ. According to Abū Hurayra and ʿAbdullāh Ibn ʿUmar ؓ, this lodging was included in the devotions of *ḥajj* and it is *sunna* for a pilgrim to camp at Abṭaḥ. However, according to ʿĀ'isha and ʿAbbās ؓ, this stay over at Abṭaḥ was coincidental and it had nothing to do with the devotions of *ḥajj*. The servants pitched his tent at that spot: that is why he camped there. Plus, it facilitated easy departure toward Madīna Munawwara.

This is where the services of a *mujtahid* or a jurist [*faqīh*] are required to sift through the various narrations and views of the Companions ؓ and award preference to one opinion over the other. The Imams have done accordingly on the basis of the following ḥadīth: "We will camp at Khayf Banī Kināna where the polytheists had vowed to oppose Islam." The Imams are of the view that this lodging was not coincidental but intentional. Allah's Messenger ﷺ intended to demonstrate the magnificence of Islam at the very spot where the disbelievers displayed their rejection [*kufr*] of Islam. Together with this objective, if other reasons are found—for example, he camped there to facilitate easy departure—this does not mean that his stay at Abṭaḥ was not intentional.

Reason 6
Underlying Causes

At times, contradictions appear due to the contradictory underlying causes found in the ḥadīths. For example, it is mentioned in a ḥadīth that Allah's Messenger ﷺ was once seated when the bier [*janāza*] of a disbeliever passed by. He immediately stood up. According to some narrations, he got up in honor of the angels accompanying the bier. If this is the case, there is even more reason for the people to stand for the passing of a Muslim bier. The narrators who consider this to be the underlying principle of the ḥadīth do not even mention the word "disbeliever" in their narrations. They do not consider it necessary because it is immaterial whether the bier is that of a Muslim or a disbeliever, due to the presence of the angels.

However, we learn from other narrations that Allah's Messenger ﷺ stood up so that the bier would not pass above the heads of the Muslims, as this is a form of humiliation to them. If this is the underlying reason for his standing up, then the practice of standing up for a *janāza* will be restricted to the bier of a disbeliever only. Hence, in this case, the word "disbeliever" must be mentioned in the ḥadīth by the narrator.

Similar is the case of another ḥadīth. Rāfiᶜ ibn Khadīj ؓ says, "We used to hire out our lands on the basis of temporary sharecropping [*muzāraᶜa*]. This was very beneficial to us but Allah's Messenger ﷺ prohibited us from it. Obedience to Allah ﷻ and His Messenger ﷺ precedes all benefits." ᶜAbdullāh ibn ᶜUmar ؓ says, "We used to hire out our plots on a temporary sharecropping basis and regarded it as beneficial and permissible. However, since Rāfiᶜ ibn Khadīj informed us that Allah's Messenger ﷺ prohibited it, we abandoned this practice."

In another narration, Rāfiᶜ ibn Khadīj ؓ says, "My uncle and other family members used to hire out their lands on a temporary sharecropping basis. The land owner and the farmer would agree that the crop which will grow around the water supply drains or any other pre-specified area will belong to the land owner while the remainder will belong to the farmer. Allah's Messenger ﷺ prohibited them from this." Rāfiᶜ ibn Khadīj ؓ was then asked, "If the land owner lets his land on a specified rental?" He replied, "That is quite in order."

In contrast to these narrations, ᶜAmr ibn Dīnar relates, "I told Tāwūs to desist from hiring out his land on the basis of sharecropping because the Companions ؓ prohibited people from doing this. Upon this Tāwūs replied, 'The most learned of the Companions, ᶜAbdullāh ibn ᶜAbbās ؓ informed me that Allah's Messenger ﷺ did not actually prohibit this practice altogether. What he actually meant was that it is better for a person to lend his plot of land to his Muslim brother for purposes of cultivation instead of letting it to him in exchange of something.'"

So, according to Ibn ᶜAbbās ؓ, the underlying cause for the prohibition was merely to ensure that people maintain good conduct with their fellow Muslim brothers. This prohibition was not a juridical injunction. However, according to Rāfiᶜ ibn Khadīj ؓ, the underlying cause of this ban was to demonstrate its prohibition and nothing else.

There are many other examples of this nature in the books of ḥadīth. We do not wish to encompass them all, nor is it our objective to do so.

In short, the narrators differ in the underlying cause for the injunction expressed in a particular ḥadīth. Each narrator will narrate the ḥadīth according to his own understanding of it. Hence, we consequently have two apparently conflicting ḥadīths.

Nevertheless, one who is confronted with both ḥadīths and is cognizant of the principles of ḥadīth, etc., is bound to grant preference to one of the narrations only and attempt to reinterpret the other. This can only be carried out by a person who knows many ḥadīths on a given subject and who also knows the actual texts of the various ḥadīths. On the other hand, a person who only knows the translation of one ḥadīth on a particular topic, has no knowledge of a contrary ḥadīth, and is not aware of the principles of awarding preference to some ḥadīths over others: will he ever be able to understand which ḥadīth is awarded preference over the other and why?

Reason 7
Words Have Multiple Meanings

One of the other reasons for the apparent contradictions in the ḥadīths is that there are many words that are sometimes used in the literal sense and at other times in the technical or figurative sense. Allah's Messenger ﷺ used to say something using a particular word in one context, while some of the Companions رضي الله عنهم considered the usage in a different context. There are not a few, but thousands of instances of this nature.

To give one example, the word *wuḍū'* is quite common in its technical sense (of ablution before prayer). However, literally, the word *wuḍū'* means cleanliness, purity, and washing of the hands. In a narration of the *Shamā'il* of Imam Tirmidhī, Salmān رضي الله عنه once told Allah's Messenger ﷺ that according to the Torah, *wuḍū'* after meals brings about blessings [*baraka*] in one's food. Allah's Messenger ﷺ added, "*Wuḍū'* before as well as after the meal is a source of blessing in one's food." In Salmān's statement as well as the statement of Allah's Messenger ﷺ, the word *wuḍū'* unanimously refers to the washing of the hands.

In addition, there is a lengthy ḥadīth narrated by ʿIkrāsh in *Sunan al-Tirmidhi*. At the end of the ḥadīth he says, "After partaking of this meal, water was brought before Allah's Messenger ﷺ. He washed his hands and thereafter rubbed them over his face and arms. He thereafter addressed me, 'O ʿIkrāsh, the injunction of making *wuḍū'* after partaking of something cooked over the fire refers to this (form of) *wuḍū'*.'" In spite of this narration being somewhat disputed [*mutakallam fīh*], we can still establish that the word *wuḍū'* is not used in its technical sense but in its literal sense.

Similarly, it is narrated in *Jamᶜ al-Fawā'id* on the authority of Bazzār that Muᶜādh ﷺ was asked, "Do you perform *wuḍū'* after partaking of something cooked over the fire?" He replied, "We wash our hands and mouth after meals and interpret it as *wuḍū'*." For this reason, all four of the Imams have unanimously agreed that the narrations which mention (the obligation of performing) *wuḍū'* after eating something cooked over the fire refers to *wuḍū'* in its literal sense (i.e. just washing the hands and mouth). Otherwise such an injunction could have been abrogated.

Likewise, on one occasion, ᶜAlī ﷺ washed a few parts (of those normally washed during *wuḍū'*) of his body. Thereafter, he commented, "This is the *wuḍū'* of one whose *wuḍū'* is still intact." Therefore, washing only a few parts of the body is not referred to as *wuḍū'* in the technical sense.

These are just a few examples where the word "*wuḍū'*" is not used in its technical sense. My aim in presenting these examples is to show that the word "*wuḍū'*" and other words have been utilized in their literal as well as their technical sense. From this, one can understand the principle cause of differences as well.

Quite frequently, certain narrators will consider the word *wuḍū'* in a certain ḥadīth in its technical sense, and they will most probably add an explanation like "*wuḍū'* such as *wuḍū'* for *ṣalāt*." This is to ensure that no doubt remains and those listening are not left in any confusion. On the other hand, if the word *wuḍū'* is not intended in its technical sense but in its literal sense, a narrator will most probably explain that it refers to the washing of the mouth and hands, etc. This is explained in order to avoid confusion.

Consequences of the Differences of the Companions

It is now clear that differences among the narrations are bound to occur. Differences among the Companions [*ṣaḥāba*] and Followers [*tābiʿīn*] will consequently bring about differences among the jurists [*fuqahā'*] as well. This is why, initially, there were differences over whether or not the consumption of anything cooked over the fire nullifies the ablution [*wuḍū'*]. However, since there were relatively very few narrations supporting its nullification in the latter times, all four Imams unanimously agreed that the ablution would not be nullified by eating something cooked over a fire.

There are many other issues on which the Imams [*ʿulama'*] and their followers disagree. One example is, the issue of whether touching the private parts nullifies the *wuḍū'* or not. Allah's Messenger ﷺ said, "Whosoever touches his private parts should perform *wuḍū'*" The Companions, Followers, and the Imams have all differed as to the type of *wuḍū'* required. According to some of them, the ḥadīth is referring to *wuḍū'* in its technical sense, while some of them assert that it refers to the literal meaning of the word. Similarly, they have differed over the meaning of the word "touch" in the aforementioned ḥadīth. Some of them say that the word "touch" refers to its literal meaning. Others say that the word "touch" refers to passing urine, because one normally touches one's private part to cleanse it after urinating. Similarly, they have differed on the status of the *wuḍū'* demanded by this ḥadīth. According to some of the jurists, *wuḍū'* is compulsory [*wājib*], while others regard this *wuḍū'* as preferable [*mustaḥab*]. This will be explained in further detail in the next chapter.

Of similar nature is a ḥadīth in which Allah's Messenger ﷺ says, "The *ṣalāt* is broken if a woman, dog, or donkey passes in front of a person performing *ṣalāt*." Some jurists take this ḥadīth literally. According to them, the *ṣalāt* is technically nullified if a woman, dog or donkey passes in front of one who is praying. However, according to other Companions ﷺ and jurists, there is no relationship between the breaking of the *ṣalāt* and the passing of one of these three. Therefore, it cannot be in taken in its literal sense. To them, the breaking of the *ṣalāt* refers to the breaking of one's concentration in the *ṣalāt*. There are not one or two, but scores of facts that affirm this second meaning. They are explained in their respective places (i.e. in books of ḥadīth commentary). We have omitted them here for the sake of brevity.

Reason 8
Different Types of Injunctions

The eighth reason for contradictory narrations is closely related to the seventh, and some aspects of it have already been alluded to in the previous chapter. In every language we find that there are various types of injunctions. Thus, when Allah's Messenger ﷺ issued a certain command, some people considered it to be compulsory, i.e. they believed in its compulsion [*wujūb*]. A second group considered it a preferable and virtuous action, while a third group regarded the injunction as merely giving permission (to perform that action).

An example of this is the ḥadīth which commands us to put water into the nostrils while performing *wuḍū'*. Taking the obvious and apparent meaning into account, some people regard this as compulsory [*wājib*], whereas another group consider it preferable, judging from other factors.

Similar in nature is another ḥadīth which makes mention of washing the hands after waking up, before making *wuḍū'*. According to some people, the apparent meaning of the ḥadīth is taken, and it is compulsory to wash the hands at that time. However, another group asserts that this is preferable [*sunna*] to wash them.

In actual fact, the reason for the differences of narrations is a long issue indeed. This matter can only be reconciled by a jurist [*faqīh*] or *mujtahid*, because wherever there is a single command, every individual is compelled to view other commands and injunctions as well. This is necessary to enable him to ascertain the status of that individual command.

If one ḥadīth makes mention of reciting the "*tashahhud*" [prayer recited in the sitting posture of *ṣalāt*] while sitting, another ḥadīth says, "Kill the snake and scorpion (if they appear before you) while performing *ṣalāt*." Obviously, both ḥadīths can not be of the same status. This is why even the Imams have differed over whether this injunction is compulsory, preferable, or merely a meritorious act.

Similarly, the Imams have differed as to whether the injunctions pertaining to the *takbīr* of *ṣalāt* or the injunction regarding the *tasbīḥ* of *rukūʿ* and *sujūd*, etc., are compulsory or merely preferable. With diligence and perseverance, all the Imams have differentiated between all of these apparently contradictory narrations, keeping in mind the ḥadīths, the actions of the Companions, and the principles of jurisprudence [*fiqh*]. Thereafter, they applied every injunction to the correct occasion. This is a clear indication of the indispensability of a *mujtahid* and the necessity of adhering to a particular school of thought.

Mere recitation of a translation of *Ṣaḥīḥ al-Bukhārī* will not enable one to determine whether a certain injunction is compulsory, optional or permissible. This is why the scholars of ḥadīth have instituted the study of the principles of Qur'ān, ḥadīth, and jurisprudence [*fiqh*] as a pre-requisite to the actual science of Qur'ān and ḥadīth. This will enable the *mujtahid* to become conscious of the various categories of Qur'ānic verses such as the general [*ʿāmm*], specified [*khāṣṣ*], ambivalent [*mujmal*], unequivocal [*mufassar*], perspicuous [*muḥkam*], interpreted [*mu'awwal*], abrogator [*nāshikh*], abrogated [*mansūkh*], etc. In addition, he should be aware of the various categories of ḥadīth such as the continuously recurrent [*mutawātir*], non-continuously recurrent [*ghayr mutawātir*], those attributed directly to the Messenger ﷺ by a Follower without mention of the Companion in between [*mursal*], continuous [*muttaṣil*], rigorously authenticated [*ṣaḥīḥ*], defective [*muʿallal*], weak [*ḍaʿīf*], etc. He should also be aware of the status of the narrators of the ḥadīths, and should be well versed in lexicography and grammar. The statements of the Companions ﷺ and the Followers, their differences, and their unanimous decisions should also be studied carefully. Apart from this, the *mujtahid* should be well acquainted with the types and categories of deduction, analogy, and logical reasoning [*qiyās*].

Reason 9
An Injunction to Sharpen the Mind

On some occasions, the Messenger of Allah ﷺ issued certain injunctions merely to sharpen the minds of his people. In other words, he wanted the people to contemplate over the injunctions he issued to them. For example, Allah's Messenger ﷺ saw a person performing *ṣalāt* while his lower garment was suspended below his ankles. He ﷺ instructed the man to repeat not only his *ṣalāt* but his *wuḍū'* as well.

On another occasion, a person performed his *ṣalāt* very haphazardly and in extreme haste. Allah's Messenger ﷺ ordered him to repeat his *ṣalāt,* saying his *ṣalāt* was not valid. He repeated his *ṣalāt* but once again, Allah's Messenger ﷺ ordered him to go and repeat his *ṣalāt.* After this happened a third time and his *ṣalāt* was still considered invalid, the person submitted, "Please explain to me. I am unable to comprehend what is required of me." Allah's Messenger ﷺ then explained to him of the repose and tranquility required in his *ṣalāt.*

Differences are bound to occur over incidents such as these because every individual who was present in such a gathering will reinterpret these commands differently. Although there are very few examples of this nature in the books of ḥadīth, they do form the basis of some of the differences in narrations.

Reason 10
Affectionate Injunctions vs Cautionary Injunctions

Allah's Messenger ﷺ was not only the Prophet of the entire community, he was also a physical doctor for the masses, a spiritual doctor to his lovers, and a leader to his people. On the one hand, he ﷺ was more affectionate than parents to a child, though he was also more proficient than an ordinary teacher and mentor in the field of spiritual nurturing and upbringing. Just as it is possible to find injunctions issued by the Messenger ﷺ in an affectionate tone, one will also come across many injunctions which were issued as stern warnings and reprimands. This is something about which there cannot be any shadow of doubt: it is a clear truth exposed to everyone. Many injunctions of Allah's Messenger ﷺ, in spite of being issued in one context, are bound to be confused with injunctions issued from the opposite context.

These factors are such that each one of them can become an individual reason for the vast differences of narrations, but our discussion is becoming inadvertently lengthy. Owing to the possible frustration of the reader, which is a consequence of lengthy discussions, I have incorporated all those reasons into one. I will terminate this discussion concisely together with a few examples.

Allah's Messenger ﷺ instructed a woman suffering from dysfunctional uterine bleeding [*mustaḥāḍa*] to take a single bath for Ẓuhr and ʿAṣr prayer, another bath for Maghrib and ʿIshā prayer, and another bath for the Fajr prayer. The Scholars have differed as to whether this type of bathing is a form of religious injunction or whether it is a form of medical treatment to combat the illness.

Similarly, one ḥadīth mentions the compulsion of *wuḍū'* after touching the private parts, while another ḥadīth says the private parts are merely a piece of the flesh of one's body. Therefore, according to this ḥadīth, just as *wuḍū'* is not compulsory after touching any other part of the body, it is not compulsory after touching the private parts. ʿAllāma Shaʿrānī (may Allah be pleased with him) explains this contradiction thus: "The non-compulsion of *wuḍū'* is for the masses only, while its compulsion is confined to the leaders of the *Umma*."

Likewise, some narrations inform us that touching a woman invalidates the *wuḍū'*, while we deduce from other narrations that the *wuḍū'* remains intact. There are conflicting opinions of the scholars in this regard and they obviously, for various conflicting reasons, either awarded preference to one narration over the other, or they established a compromise between the two conflicting narrations. ʿAllāma Shaʿrānī (may Allah be pleased with him) correlated between these two ḥadīths in the method demonstrated above. He ruled that the first ḥadīth applies to the leaders while the second is for the general masses.

In one battle, Allah's Messenger ﷺ said, "Whoever kills a non-Muslim on the battlefield is entitled to the goods in the possession of the non-Muslim." According to some scholars, this injunction is more of a political or diplomatic nature than a religious injunction. Allah's Messenger ﷺ issued this statement as a king would issue a royal statement. Hence, if the leader of the Muslim army wishes to issue such a statement, he may do so if he feels it is expedient. Conversely, some scholars assert that this was a religious injunction. They argue that it will always be applicable and can not be subjected to the discretion of the leader. There are thousands of ḥadīths dealing with jihad which are perfect examples of the differences in narrations.

In addition, there are many narrations which prohibit his companions from certain farming arrangements. This prohibition stems from the Messenger of Allah's ﷺ affection toward the farm laborers. (This prohibition is not general, since most forms of farming are permitted in the *Sharīʿa*.)

In a similar vein, many people were prevented from excessive fasting on grounds of the Messenger of Allah's ﷺ affection for them. ʿAbdullāh ibn ʿAmr ؓ reports that Allah's Messenger ﷺ once told him, "I have been informed that you fast daily and you observe optional [*nafl*] prayer throughout the night." He replied, "This is indeed the case." Allah's Messenger ﷺ thereupon said, "Do not do this. You should fast on certain days and refrain on certain days. You should perform *ṣalāt* during a portion of the night and sleep during a portion of it as well. Your body also has a right over you. If you continue doing as I advised you, you will not get tired. Your family also has a right over you. Set aside some time for them during the day and night. Your friends, relatives and visitors also have a right over you. Therefore, fasting only three days a month and completing the recitation of the Holy Qur'ān only once every month will suffice for you."

ᶜAbdullāh replied, "Oh Messenger of Allah! I can manage much more than that." Following repeated requests, the Messenger of Allah ﷺ finally relented and said, "Fine! I will permit you no more than the fast of Dāwūd ﵇: You may fast every alternate day and no more. Also, you are prohibited from completing the Holy Qur'ān more than once every seven days."

This ḥadīth has been transmitted with slight variations in its text in the various books of ḥadīth. According to the version mentioned in the *Mishkāt al-Maṣābīḥ* on the authority of Imam Bukhārī, the ḥadīth prohibits perpetual fasting. At the end of the narration, what else save affection for ᶜAbdullāh ﵁ had prompted Allah's Messenger ﷺ to permit him to fast the fast of Dāwūd (i.e. to fast every alternate day)? This is why ᶜAbdullāh ﵁ used to lament in his old and feeble age, "If only I had taken heed of the advice of Allah's Messenger ﷺ."

Compelling Interpretations

There are many other ḥadīths which were conveyed as threats or admonishments. For example, Allah's Messenger ﷺ said, "There is no fast for one who observes perpetual fasting [*ṣawm al-dahr*]." According to some scholars, this ḥadīth is more of an admonishment to abstain from perpetual fasting. It does not mean that (one who does this) will not be rewarded for it, or that his fasting is null and void.

Likewise, Allah's Messenger ﷺ cautions, "A believer [*mu'min*] does not remain a believer while he is committing adultery, nor does he remain a believer while he is stealing." Of a similar nature is the ḥadīth wherein Allah's Messenger ﷺ says, "Whosoever consumes alcohol, his *ṣalāt* is not accepted for forty days."

The aforementioned reasons for the differences of narrations were merely mentioned as examples. This category (of differences) is not confined to these examples only. All I wish to prove at this juncture is that the basis for which these differences came about is indispensable. All the reasons for the differences cannot be accommodated in this brief assignment nor, due to my helplessness, do I wish to cover them all. The objective of this assignment has been achieved up to a certain degree, in that the apparent contradictions in the statements of Allah's Messenger ﷺ are all explainable. From among the many reasons for these differences, some have already been explained above as examples.

At this point, I would like to discuss other reasons for these differences which surfaced in the era of the Companions ﷺ, and the consequent differences that appeared. I will also present a few examples from these eras. Before I go any further, though, I would like to bring up an unfounded objection (which normally comes up) at this juncture.

Other Aspects
Two Categories of Laws

An objection which normally appears at this juncture is this: since Allah's Messenger ﷺ was sent to this world to convey the injunctions of Islamic law [*Sharīʿa*], and this was a primary reason for his advent, why did he not convey all the injunctions of *Sharīʿa* in complete detail during his lifetime? This would have averted the confusion and anxiety of contradictory narrations and other such issues.

On the outside, this objection looks quite clear-cut and sensible, but in reality it is unfounded and baseless. This objection stems from a lack of insight into the laws of *Sharīʿa*. In actual fact, it is due to an intense degree of affection toward this *Umma* that Allah's Messenger ﷺ did not regulate and gather all of the by-laws of the *Sharīʿa,* since this would have caused hardships to the *Umma*. Instead, he ﷺ divided the laws of the *Sharīʿa* into two categories: a set of laws in which contemplation, deliberation and discussion has been abhorred, and a second set of laws in which differences of opinions have been declared a source of Allah's ﷻ mercy. Thus, every action, even if the action is incorrect, can potentially earn the reward of Allah ﷻ, provided that the error is not due to one's negligence.

In essence, the *Sharīʿa* has divided all the laws into two basic categories: the definitive [*qaṭʿī*] and the speculative [*ẓannī*]. *Qaṭʿī* is a reference to those laws which are not left to the intellectual capabilities of man. They are all explicit, definitive, and unequivocal, and man has no right to reinterpret or to re-expound these laws. Anyone reinterpreting these laws is in error and would be considered misguided. The second set of laws is such that the *Sharīʿa* has placed no constraints upon them. In fact, this set of laws has taken into account the weakness of the *Umma* and is intended to make things simpler for the people. The one who reinterprets these laws differently and does not practice them will not be considered misguided. The first set of laws is referred to as fundamental beliefs [*iʿtiqādāt*], while the second set is referred to as by-laws or derived laws [*juz'iyyāt* or *farʿiyyāt*].

Under the category of by-laws, the *Sharīʿa* did not place any constraints. If all the fundamentals, compulsions, etc., were explained in complete detail by Allah's Messenger ﷺ, everything in this category would have also been incorporated in the first category. This would have consequently placed hardships on the *Umma*. Plus, even if this was the case, it would still have been extremely difficult to preserve these laws from differences of opinion. Differences would still have occurred because all statements constituting the by-laws of *Sharīʿa* are issued through the medium of words. Words are multi-facetted and can have multiple interpretations. Hence, the *Sharīʿa* has divided the laws into the two categories of fundamentals and by-laws, and made it strictly prohibited to debate on the first category as is evident from the following verse:

> Allah has established for you the same religion as that which He enjoined upon Nūḥ, and that which We had revealed to you and that which We have enjoined upon Ibrāhīm, Mūsā, and ʿĪsā; namely that you should remain steadfast in religion and make no divisions therein (*Surat al-Shūrā* 42, 13).

This verse sternly prohibits any debate in religion [*dīn*] with regard to the first category of injunctions. However, differences in the second category are considered a source of mercy upon mankind. This is why there has been no prohibition on this type of debate and differences, as evident from the scores of incidents which occurred during the blessed era of Allah's Messenger ﷺ. I will present just two examples of this nature.

In one example, Imam Nasāʾī (may Allah be pleased with him) narrates on the authority of Ṭāriq an incident of two Companions ۞ who were both in need of a compulsory bath [*ghusl*]. Due to a lack of water, one of them refrained completely from performing *ṣalāt* while the other performed *tayammum* [dry ablution]. On their return to Allah's Messenger ﷺ, he approved both of their actions.

Similarly, on another occasion, the Messenger of Allah ﷺ commanded a group of Companions ۞ to perform their ʿAṣr prayer at the dwellings of Banū Qurayẓa. Some of them took the command to perform the ʿAṣr prayer at Banū Qurayẓa literally and acted accordingly. Even though their *ṣalāt* was delayed from its actual time, they nonetheless executed what they felt was the meaning of the command issued to them by Allah's Messenger ﷺ. However, another group regarded this as a command to reach Banū Qurayẓa in haste (i.e. by ʿAṣr time). Hence, they performed their ʿAṣr *ṣalāt* at its proper time, en-route to Banū Qurayẓa. Allah's Messenger ﷺ did not object to the actions of either of the two groups. This incident is mentioned in detail in *Ṣaḥīḥ al-Bukhārī*. There are numerous other incidents of this nature.

Fundamental and Subsidiary Differences

In short, there is a vast distinction between fundamental differences and secondary differences. Those who consider these secondary differences equal to the fundamental differences and apply the Qur'ānic verses and ḥadīths about the evil of differences to these secondary differences are either ignorant or fooled into believing otherwise. There is no doubt that the *Sharīʿa* has placed great ease and flexibility on these secondary differences. If this was not the case, the *Umma* would have been encumbered with difficulties beyond their endurance. This was one of the reasons why Imam Mālik (may Allah be pleased with him) declined to comply with Caliph Hārūn al-Rashīd's request for him to hang a copy of his *Muwaṭṭa'* upon the wall of the Kaʿba and issue a command for everyone to adhere to it, in order to ensure that people did not differ over religious [*dīnī*] matters. Imam Mālik was requested repeatedly to do this but he emphatically refused each time and declared:

> The Companions ﷺ also differed in subsidiary issues and all of them were considered to be correct. Their statements and schools of thought are practiced throughout the world and there is no sense in prohibiting the people from other schools of thought.

Similarly, when Caliph Manṣūr went for *ḥajj*, he requested Imam Mālik (may Allah be pleased with him) to give him a copy of all his works so that he (Manṣūr) could have them published and dispatched to all the parts of the Islamic world. Manṣūr wanted all the Muslims to adhere to a uniform code of Islamic law. Imam Mālik (may Allah be pleased with him) replied,

> O leader of the faithful! Do not ever think of doing this. The people have in their possession the ḥadīths and the statements of the Companions ﷺ, which they are adhering to. Allow them to continue accordingly.

Differences: A Source of Mercy

This is a desired objective of the statement of Allah's Messenger ﷺ wherein he says, "The differences of my *Umma* are a source of mercy." The fact that these differences of opinion are a source of mercy is quite obvious. Every Imam has some difference or another on subsidiary issues of *Sharīʿa.* In addition, it is permissible to issue a religious verdict [*fatwā*] according to the school of thought of another Imam provided there is a legal and juridical [*sharʿī*] need to do so. However, if there were no allowances for such differences of opinion, it would not be permissible to sway from one ruling to another even if there was a dire need for it.

In short, the differences of opinion found among the Imams are religiously required, and the benefits of them are manifold. Allah willing, if time assists me in my endeavors, I will mention this topic in more detail while discussing the differences of opinion of the third era. It is not my objective of discussion at this point. Those who have some inclination toward jurisprudence [*fiqh*] will surely understand the aforementioned benefits of the differences of opinion.

Prejudice Toward any School

ʿAllāma Shaʿrānī (may Allah be pleased with him) writes in his book *Al-Mīzān,*

> If you view it with an impartial eye, you will clearly realize that all the four Imams and their followers are on the path of divine guidance. Once you have studied this carefully, you will not have objections against the

followers of any of the Imams. It will be firmly impressed on your mind that all the four schools of thought are part and parcel of the *Sharīʿa*, and that the contradictory statements of the various Imams are a source of divine mercy. Allah ﷻ is All-Knowing and All-Wise and His expediency demanded that things should turn out as they have become. If Allah ﷻ abhorred this difference of opinion, then He would have forbidden it as He had forbidden debating on the fundamental teachings of the *Sharīʿa*. If you regard the subsidiary differences of opinion as the same as fundamental differences in religion [*dīn*], you will land yourself in an abyss of destruction because Allah's Messenger ﷺ concluded that differences in subsidiary issues of religion are a source of divine mercy.

In actual fact, the various opinions of the Imams are all extracted from the ḥadīths. The only differences between the opinions of the Imams is that, where one Imam considers a certain juridical [*sharʿī*] injunction as compulsory, another would consider the same as optional. By this statement, I am in no way implying that one is at liberty to select the opinion of whichever Imam one fancies—either the compulsory or the optional. Some students were duped into believing that this is what I meant. This is most definitely not what I mean, as it would render the entire religion a plaything. What I am saying is that each of the Imams has selected one of the two options before him. However, whichever one they select, their followers are bound to adhere to it.

Whatever I have mentioned about the Imams I have not said simply because I cherish favorable thoughts about them. On the contrary, I have established good thoughts toward them as a result of extensive research into their opinions, deductions, inferences, and corroborating statements. Whoever does not believe me should study my book, *Al-Manhaj al-mubīn fī adillat al-mujtahidīn* [The Clear Way in the Proofs of the Mujtahids]. I have assembled all the corroborating statements of the various Imams in that book and, consequently, established that they were all divinely guided.

The fact of the matter is that as long as one does not cross all the stations of the spiritual path [*sulūk*] through the companionship and direction of an accomplished spiritual guide [*shaykh kāmil*], the complete reality of this, as it should be understood, will not be exposed to him. Hence, if you wish to savor its taste, you should also proceed to an accomplished spiritual guide and exert yourself in order to acquire the reality of these

> matters. This is not a fabrication from myself, but an established reality confirmed by the statements of the learned elders [*mashā'ikh*].
>
> Shaykh Muḥyī 'l-Dīn ibn ʿArabī writes in his book *Futūḥāt al-Makkiyya,* "When a person is bound to a particular school of thought and he also progresses in the field of spirituality, at the very summit he reaches a sea (of consciousness) through which all the Imams have passed. At that time a person realizes that all the schools of thought are on the right path. This can be likened to a Prophet who, once he receives divine revelation [*waḥy*], has a good view of all the other religions as well."

This priceless treatise of Imam Shaʿrānī (may Allah be pleased with him), which runs into almost a hundred pages, is worth writing in gold. His topic is extremely beneficial; in fact, the entire work is worth translating.

In short, what I wish to say is that the differences of opinion found among the Imams which appear to be disunity are in actual fact not disunity. Whatever their stages of differences, they are indispensable and their absence would have been a burden on the *Umma.* Furthermore, since their differences of opinion stem from the differences in narrations, there was a religious [*dīnī*] need to have the narrations also revealed with some amount of ambiguity. If these juridical laws were conclusively revealed like the fundamental tenets of faith, there would be no scope for the Imams to have any differences. In that case, any debate of the Imams would have been a source of misguidance and the lack of debate would have caused untold hardship to the community at large.

Nonetheless, this does not mean that a person is at liberty to infer and draw conclusions from the texts of the Qur'ān or ḥadīths according to his own understanding, as this would lead him astray. Such a difference of opinion is not sound. The only difference of opinion which is reputable is that which is subjected to juridical [*sharʿī*] maxims and principles. For instance, in the incident which dealt with bathing when in a seminally defiled state [*janāba*], Allah's Messenger ﷺ considered the actions of those who had speculated based to their own understanding as ignorance.

Part Two

The Era of the Companions & Followers

رضي الله عنهم

Reason 1
Narration by Meaning

Apart from the reasons mentioned regarding the first era, there were many other factors during the era of the Companions and Followers that contributed to the conflict in narrations. This conflict was bound to occur.

One of the foremost reasons for these conflicting narrations is due to narration by meaning and not narration by actual text. In other words, people used to narrate the ḥadīths in their own words and not in the actual words of Allah's Messenger ﷺ. Ibn Sīrīn says, "I used to hear one ḥadīth from ten people and all of them used to differ in the text but they used to be unanimous in the meaning."

ʿAllāma Dhahabī (may Allah be pleased with him) quotes the statement of Abū Hātim in his book *Tadhkirat al-ḥuffāz:* "I have not seen any of the ḥadīth narrators, besides Qubaysa, memorizing and relating the exact words of the ḥadīths (as they had heard them) without any change whatsoever."

ʿAllāma Suyūṭī (may Allah be pleased with him) has dealt with this topic in detail in his book *Tadrīb al-rāwī,* wherein he also transmits the various opinions of the scholars on this issue of whether or not narrating the meaning of the ḥadīth instead of the actual text is permissible. However, ʿAllāma Suyūṭī says that all four Imams have unanimously agreed that narrating a ḥadīth by meaning instead of the actual text is permissible, provided the other prerequisites are found in the narrator. He based its permissibility on a ḥadīth narrated by Ṭabarānī and Ibn Manda in which ʿAbdullāh ibn Sulaymān ﷺ once told the Messenger of Allah ﷺ that he was unable to narrate the Messenger's ﷺ exact words. The Messenger ﷺ permitted him to change the text of the ḥadīth, provided he narrated the meaning of the ḥadīth in full.

The Difficulty of Narrating by Memory

It is also very difficult to remember all the actual words of the ḥadīths. On one occasion Makhūl asked Wāthila ibn al-Asqaᶜ ﷺ to narrate a ḥadīth that he heard from Allah's Messenger ﷺ without adding or subtracting any words and without a doubt or error in the text of the ḥadīth. Wāthila asked him, "Does any one of you know the Qur'ān by heart?" Makhūl replied, "We do not know the Qur'ān so well that we would not make any mistakes whatsoever." Upon this Wāthila commented, "The Holy Qur'ān is written out and preserved in its original form. In spite of this, you tend to make errors in the letter *"fā"* and *"wāw"* (i.e. they are sometimes interchanged), etc. So how can I narrate a ḥadīth in the manner you have requested? In fact, some of the ḥadīths I have only heard once. When it comes to narrating the ḥadīths of Allah's Messenger ﷺ, consider the narration of the meaning as sufficient (and do not be overly concerned with the actual text)." Wakīᶜ (may Allah be pleased with him) said, "If there were no (allowance for) narrating the meaning of the ḥadīths instead of the actual text, the entire nation of Muslims would have been destroyed."

According to Ibn al-ᶜArabī, narrating the meaning of the ḥadīths rather than their text was permissible only for the Companions ﷺ, and not for anybody else. However, other ḥadīth scholars [*muḥaddithīn*] like Qāsim ibn Muḥammad, Ibn Sīrīn, Zuhrī, Ibrāhīm (al-Nakhᶜay), Shaᶜbī, among others have permitted this for all narrators, albeit with certain conditions.

This was one of the main reasons why a great multitude of the Followers [*tābiᶜīn*] abstained from attributing a ḥadīth directly to the Messenger of Allah ﷺ. Instead, they used to narrate the ḥadīth in the form of an injunction.

Among others, the aforementioned issue is one of the chief reasons why Imam Abū Ḥanīfa (may Allah be pleased with him) refrained from attributing the ḥadīths directly to Allah's Messenger ﷺ, along with the fact that it is dangerous to attribute (a ḥadīth) directly to him. It is possible that in narrating the meaning instead of the actual text, one may attribute something incorrectly to him and consequently become liable to severe punishment.

Caution in Textual Narrations

Other great scholars were also very cautious about attributing the ḥadīths directly to Allah's Messenger ﷺ because it was extremely difficult to abstain from any form of error or mistakes while narrating the actual (text of the) ḥadīths.

Even a personality like Ibn Masᶜūd ؓ was extremely cautious in attributing any ḥadīth directly to Allah's Messenger ﷺ. He was one of the greatest of the Companions ؓ, about whom Abū Mūsā al-Ashᶜarī ؓ says, "He (ᶜAbdullāh ibn Masᶜūd) used to frequent the house of Allah's Messenger ﷺ to such an extent that we were initially under the impression that he was a family member." Allah's Messenger ﷺ even granted him permission to listen to his personal secrets. During his lifetime, the Messenger of Allah ﷺ appointed him ؓ as a teacher of the Holy Qur'ān. The Messenger ﷺ once said, "If I were to appoint anyone as a leader [*amīr*], I would have appointed Ibn Masᶜūd as a leader."

Ḥadīths like this explaining the virtues of Ibn Masᶜūd are rarely found narrated in favor of the other Companions ؓ. This is why Imam Abū Ḥanīfa (may Allah be pleased with him) decided to make the religious verdicts [*fatāwā*] of Ibn Masᶜūd the basis of (much of) his jurisprudence [*fiqh*]. We will explain this in detail at another time.

What I wish to make clear at this point is that in spite of his excessive knowledge, his lofty virtues, and his numerous ḥadīths, he rarely attributed the ḥadīths directly to Allah's Messenger ﷺ. Abū ᶜAmr al-Shaybānī says, "I stayed with ʿAbdullāh ibn Masʿūd ﷺ for a period of one year and I did not hear him attributing any ḥadīth to the Messenger of Allah ﷺ. If he did, per chance, say 'Allah's Messenger ﷺ said' in regards to any sentence, his entire body would tremble (out of fear of attributing something incorrectly to him)."

Anas ﷺ, the special attendant [*khādim khāṣṣ*] of Allah's Messenger ﷺ, says, "If I did not have a fear of slipping up, I would have narrated many ḥadīths that I had heard from Allah's Messenger ﷺ. However, I fear that if I narrate those ḥadīths, I will fall under the threat of punishment."

Suhayb ﷺ says: "I will be able to narrate the incidents that took place in our battles while we were with Allah's Messenger ﷺ. However, for me to narrate that 'this is what Allah's Messenger ﷺ said,' I will not be able to do that."

In short, there are many such incidents which highlight the Companions' ﷺ caution when it came to attributing the ḥadīths to Allah's Messenger ﷺ. If Allah ﷻ wills, I will deal with this in more detail when we discuss the allegations against Imam Abū Ḥanīfa (may Allah ﷻ be pleased with him) regarding his knowledge of ḥadīth. At this point, I have mentioned a few incidents to elucidate on the fact that, since it was difficult to narrate the ḥadīths word for word, the narrators related the meanings of the ḥadīths instead. I have also explained why the senior Companions ﷺ refrained from attributing anything directly to Allah's Messenger ﷺ.

Since we have established the permissibility of narrating (a ḥadīth) with meaning instead of narrating with the actual text, we have also established that differences in those narrations are also inevitable. Due to a difference in interpretation, differences in meaning are also bound to appear. This is one of the reasons why Abū Bakr ﷺ, in his speech after the death of Allah's Messenger ﷺ, forbade the people from narrating ḥadīths, as this would have created differences and contention among the community.

Reason 2
Abrogation

One of the other reasons for differences in narrations during the era of the Companions and Followers ﷺ was that many a time Allah's Messenger ﷺ would say something which later became abrogated. However, some of the people who heard the initial injunction were probably not present to hear its abrogation and thus continued narrating what they heard (before the abrogation). For example, there are many narrations which permit wiping [*masaḥ*] over the turban. However, Imam Muḥammad al-Shaybānī (may Allah be pleased with him) writes in his *Muwaṭṭa'*, "As far as we are aware, wiping over the turban was permissible at the very beginning of Islam and it was later prohibited."

Similarly, he narrates the statement of Abū Saʿīd al-Khudrī ﷺ that bathing [*ghusl*] is compulsory upon every mature person on Fridays. However, Ibn ʿAbbās ﷺ said, "This compulsion was confined to the beginning of Islam only. At that time the people used to work in their fields themselves and were unable to employ any servants due to extreme poverty. Their garments were made of thick woolen material at that time. While toiling in their fields, due to excessive perspiration, their clothing used to give off an offensive odor. The *masjid* in those times was also very small. When all the people used to gather in the *masjid* for the Friday prayer, the odor given off by some people used to be very offensive to other attendees. This is why they were commanded to have a bath and apply perfume, etc. Thereafter, Allah ﷻ provided ease for the Muslims and the *masjid* was also extended. Hence, the compulsion of bathing no longer remains."

There is also a comparable narration from Abū Hurayra ﷺ which says that the *wuḍū'* is nullified if one consumes anything cooked over the fire. Contrary to this, Jābir ﷺ relates, "Toward the latter part of his life, the Messenger of Allah's ﷺ habit was not to make *wuḍū'* after eating something cooked over the fire." This ḥadīth clearly shows that the compulsion of *wuḍū'* was abrogated. However, Imam Abū Dāwūd (may Allah be pleased with him) disagrees with this interpretation of the ḥadīth. This is why we also mentioned another interpretation of this ḥadīth previously [*see page* 21]: the word *wuḍū'* in the ḥadīth of Abū Hurayra ﷺ (as explained above) refers to the washing of the hands and the mouth and not to the technical meaning of *wuḍū'*.

Reason 3
The Problem of Human Error

The scholars are unanimous in their view that the Companions ﷺ were all reliable narrators [*ʿadūl*]. They can neither be criticized nor censured. In his *Iṣāba,* Ibn Ḥajar al-ʿAsqalānī describes this as the unanimous opinion of the People of the Sunna [*Ahl al-Sunna*]. However, everyone is afflicted with forgetfulness, errors and other human shortcomings. Hence, there is a possibility of making a mistake while narrating a ḥadīth.

I have already mentioned the statement of ʿImrān ibn Ḥusayn ﷺ, in which he says, "By Allah! I know so many ḥadīths that I can go on narrating for a very long time. However, I am restrained by the fact that there are some Companions who heard the ḥadīths from Allah's Messenger ﷺ like I did, but in spite of this they are prone to making mistakes while narrating. Obviously, they are not doing this intentionally. If I had to narrate, I fear I would also fall into the same abyss."

Likewise, whenever ʿAlī ﷺ would hear a ḥadīth from anyone other than Abū Bakr ﷺ, he used to make the narrator swear an oath that he had reported it exactly the way he heard it from Allah's Messenger ﷺ.

The inevitable existence of these types of errors explains why, among other things, it is incumbent to compare narrations with one another to determine if there are any errors. If there are any contradictions on the part of the narrator, the contradictions will be resolved.

The specialists in the field of ḥadīth have prohibited the people from acting upon the ḥadīths directly until they have the capability to distinguish between the authentic and the unauthentic, between the correct and the incorrect, and between the truth and the fabricated.

There are scores of examples of such errors in the books of ḥadīth. One such example involves a narration from ʿAbdullāh ibn ʿUmar ﷺ which states that Allah's Messenger ﷺ performed *ʿumra* in the month of Rajab. When ʿĀ'isha ﷺ heard of his account, she said, "Ibn ʿUmar ﷺ has forgotten. Allah's Messenger ﷺ did not perform any *ʿumra* in the month of Rajab."

In addition, we have already previously mentioned the case in which ʿAbdullāh ibn ʿUmar ﷺ said, "The deceased is punished in his grave if his family cries or mourns over him." His report was rejected by ʿĀ'isha ﷺ, who insisted that Ibn ʿUmar ﷺ had erred in narrating the ḥadīth. According to her, the ḥadīth is as follows: "On one occasion, Allah's Messenger ﷺ passed by a deceased Jewish woman who was being mourned over by her family members. He remarked, 'These people are crying over her whereas she is being inflicted with the punishment of the grave!'" According to ʿĀ'isha ﷺ, their crying had nothing to do with her punishment.

Likewise, Abū Hurayra ﷺ says if a person is in need of a compulsory bath [*ghusl*] at the time of true dawn [*ṣubḥ ṣādiq*], he is not permitted to fast on that specific day. He narrates this (ruling) from Allah's Messenger ﷺ, and this was also his personal ruling [*fatwā*] on the issue. Such narrations are compiled in detail in *Fatḥ al-Bārī,* the commentary on *Ṣaḥīḥ al-Bukhārī,* under the chapter dealing with fasting. However, in opposition to this, ʿĀ'isha and Umm Salama ﷺ report that at times the Messenger ﷺ used to be in need of bathing [*ghusl*] at dawn, but he would fast on those days as well.

Similarly, a group of narrators relate that the *ṣalāt* is nullified if a woman or dog passes in front of one performing *ṣalāt.* ʿĀ'isha ﷺ rejected this view, saying this narration is incorrect.

Finally, Fāṭima bint Qays ﷺ narrated that a woman who has been issued an irrevocable divorce has no right to claim food, clothing, or shelter from her husband. When ʿUmar ﷺ heard this he remarked, "How can I relinquish a Qur'ānic verse for the statement of one woman?"

To sum up, one of the reasons for the contradiction of narrations stems from the differences in how the ḥadīths were preserved. At times, those narrating the ḥadīths tended to slip up in their narrations. This is not impossible. Sometimes, even the most intelligent person can become confused with comprehending, transmitting, or relating the meaning of a statement. There are many such cases in which the narrators erred in spite of being reliable and truthful. This is why the scholars have laid down stringent rules for accepting the narration of a lone narrator. One of the rules is to compare the narration with other narrations. If it is conforming to the juridical principles, it will be accepted; otherwise it will not.

The aforementioned incident of ʿUmar ﷺ also supports one of the principles of the Ḥanafī school. According to the Ḥanafīs, the ḥadīth that is in greater conformance with the Qur'ān will be awarded preference over the ḥadīth that is not as conforming to it, even if the latter has relatively more reliable narrators or there are other narrations supporting it.

All of these incidents also verify what I have repeatedly indicated: that the only person who can practice upon the ḥadīth directly is the one who has the capacity to recognize right from wrong. It is quite bewildering to note that to determine the purity of gold, one avails himself of the services of a bullion dealer, but to practice upon the ḥadīths, he considers the services of an analyst as dispensable. The one who does this is quite proud of his own knowledge in spite of his ignorance. We beseech the assistance of Allah ﷻ alone.

Reason 4
Love for Allah's Messenger ﷺ

The Companions ﷺ were the real devotees and ardent followers of Allah's Messenger ﷺ. They were prepared to lay down a hundred lives for every action of his. They were wholly befitting of the poem:

If the Almighty had to bestow me with unlimited hearts,
I would have sacrificed a hundred for every action.

The relationship the Companions ﷺ enjoyed with Allah's Messenger ﷺ cannot be expressed in words. Every one of the most seemingly trivial incidents that transpired while they were in the company of the Messenger ﷺ is a testament to their devotion to him.

Anas ﷺ narrates, "The Messenger of Allah ﷺ passed by the house of a Companion who had added an additional room to it. Allah's Messenger ﷺ asked who the house belonged to. On being informed, the Messenger ﷺ did not utter a word. When the Companion in question appeared before Allah's Messenger ﷺ, he ﷺ declined to reply to his *salām*. The Companion ﷺ made *salām* many times, but to no avail. When informed by the others about what had transpired earlier, he immediately went home and demolished the extended room. Above that, he did not even inform Allah's Messenger ﷺ of his action: out of shame and remorse, he refrained from informing him ﷺ. The Messenger of Allah ﷺ only learnt of it when he happened to pass by the same house on another occasion."

The Companions ﷺ used to accept even the outward meaning of the words of Allah's Messenger ﷺ. They at times were quite aware that this was not what he meant, but taking the literal words into account, they used to adhere to it.

Once, Allah's Messenger ﷺ pointed to one of the doors of the *masjid* [*al-Nabawī*] and remarked, "It would have been a good idea to reserve this door for the exclusive use of the women." From then on, ʿAbdullāh ibn ʿUmar ﷺ never entered the *masjid* by that door.

Likewise, when Abū Saʿīd al-Khudrī ﷺ was on his death-bed, he called for a new set of clothes and put them on. He thereafter said, "I heard Allah's Messenger ﷺ saying that a person will be resurrected on the Day of Judgment with the clothing he dies in." On the contrary, it has been established by famous ḥadīths that everyone will be resurrected naked on the Day of Judgment. This is discussed under the commentary of the Qur'ānic verse, "As We commenced the initial creation, so shall We return it" (*Surat al-Anbiyā'* 21:104). This meaning is established on the grounds of many ḥadīths. It would be preposterous to suggest that Abū Sa'īd al-Khudrī ؓ was unaware of the meaning of the ḥadīths. He was aware of it, but he chose to act on the literal meaning of the ḥadīth and wear the new clothes.

The books of ḥadīth are replete with such examples. On the surface, these examples seem dubious, but one who has "had a sip from the fountains of love" will clearly understand the importance of even the apparent words of his beloved, above and beyond the consideration of their actual meaning. This was one of the main reasons why the Companions ؓ used to narrate even the abrogated ḥadīths.

On the outside, it seems senseless to propagate abrogated ḥadīths (but such was their love for the Messenger ﷺ and his words). Similarly, there are many such ḥadīths which were narrated in spite of the fact that their apparent meanings were unanimously declared obsolete.

From this, we understand why the ḥadīth scholars have laid down such stringent rules and regulations for acquiring the science of ḥadīth, and why they were so cautious before saying or writing anything on this subject. They have even laid down principles and conditions for the seekers of this science. The rules and regulations set out for the teachers and ḥadīth scholars are even more stringent.

The Advice of Imam Bukhārī to the Seeker of Ḥadīth

Even though the issue at hand is growing more long-winded, spurred by the necessity of the present discussion, I will narrate a remarkable quote from Imam Bukhārī (may Allah be pleased with him) which will enlighten the reader on the diligence required to become a seeker of ḥadīth, let alone an accomplished *shaykh* or scholar of ḥadīth [*muḥaddith*].

ʿAllāma Suyūṭī relates (through his chain) that Muḥammad ibn Aḥmad said: "When Abū 'l-ʿAbbās Walīd ibn Ibrāhīm was deposed as the chief justice of Rayy (formally of the great cities of Persia located a few miles from Tehran) and he came to Bukhārā, my teacher, Abū Ibrāhīm Al-Khatallī took me with him to see Walīd. My teacher requested him to narrate those ḥadīths to me which he had heard from his teachers [*mashā'ikh*]. He replied, 'I have not heard anything from them.' My teacher was quite shocked and remarked, 'How can you say that you have not heard anything from them whereas you are a deeply-read scholar?'

Walīd then related his story saying, 'When I became a rational and mature adult and I developed a passion toward the science of ḥadīth, I went to Imam Bukhārī (may Allah be pleased with him) and explained my intentions to him. He advised me thus, "Son, before you set out to pursue any field, make sure you are well-grounded with its prerequisites and demands. And remember that a person cannot become a perfect scholar in the science of ḥadīth [*muḥaddith*] until and unless he writes four things with four other things, which are as indispensable as four things, which resemble four other things. (He must write these things) in four times, with four conditions, in four places, upon four things, from four types of people, and for four objectives. All of these four-angled things can only be achieved with another four things coupled with another four. Once all these things are achieved, four things will become insignificant before him and he will be tried with four other things. If he exercises patience in these four trials, Allah ﷻ will honor him with four things in this world and award him four things in the hereafter."

I said, "May Allah ﷻ have mercy upon you. Please explain these four-angled things for me." He said, "Certainly. The four things he has to write are:

(1) the statements and commands of Allah's Messenger ﷺ.

(2) the sayings of the Companions ؓ and their relative ranks,
(3) the sayings of the Followers ؓ and their ranks (i.e. who among them are reliable and who are not), and
(4) the conditions of all the narrators who narrate ḥadīths.

These (four pieces of information) must be written together with the following four things:

(1) the actual names of the narrators,
(2) their appellations or titles [*kunā*],
(3) their places of residence, and
(4) their dates of birth and death (to determine whether the narrator actually met the people he has narrated from).

(These are indispensable to him) just (as four things are necessary with four other things:)

(1) as praises [*taḥmīd*] of Allah ﷻ (are necessary) with the *khuṭba*,
(2) as salutations [*ṣalawāt*], (are necessary) with mention of the name of Allah's Messenger ﷺ.
(3) as (the recitation of) *bismillāh* (is necessary) with a *sūra* (of the Qur'ān), and
(4) as the *takbīr* (is necessary) with the *ṣalāt*.

These resemble four other things (which are names of four categories of ḥadīth):

(1) the *musnadāt* [narrations traceable to the Messenger ﷺ],
(2) the *mursalāt* [narrations transmitted by a Follower from the Messenger ﷺ directly without a Companion in between],
(3) the *mawqūfāt* [narrations traceable only to a Companion ؓ], and
(4) the *maqṭūʿāt* [narrations traceable only to a Follower].

(These things must all be written) in four times:

(1) in his childhood,

(2) in his age of discernment (i.e. close to maturity),
(3) in his youth, and
(4) in his old age.

(In other words, he must continue acquiring ḥadīths at all times throughout every stage of his life. They must be written) under four conditions:

(1) while his is occupied,
(2) while he is free,
(3) in his poverty, and
(4) in his affluence.

(In other words, he must diligently pursue the knowledge of these things no matter what his circumstances may be. This is done) at four places:

(1) in mountainous terrain,
(2) on the seas,
(3) in cities, and
(4) in rural areas.

(In other words, he must endeavor to acquire this science from the right teacher, no matter where that teacher is located. He writes what he has acquired) upon four things:

(1) upon stones,
(2) upon shells,
(3) upon skins, and
(4) upon bones.

(In other words, even when he does not find paper he will continue recording it somewhere) until he finds the paper upon which to preserve it. (He acquires it from four different types of people:)

(1) from his seniors,
(2) from his juniors,
(3) from his counterparts, and

(4) from the books of his father, provided he has firm conviction that these are his father's books.

(In other words, he endeavors to acquire this science in every way possible without feeling ashamed to obtain it even from his juniors. He has four objectives for doing all of these things:)

(1) to acquire (this science) solely for the pleasure of Allah ﷻ,
(2) to practice upon the ḥadīths which conform to the verses of the Holy Qur'ān,
(3) to propagate (the science) to those who seek it, and
(4) to write it out so that it can be a source of guidance to those who will come after him.

Thereafter, the aforementioned four things cannot be acquired (unless he has first acquired) four other things that are part of human acquisition:

(1) the knowledge of how to read and write,
(2) lexicography and vocabulary,
(3) morphology, and
(4) syntax,

together with four other things that are not of human acquisition, but are bestowed by Allah ﷻ:

(1) sound health,
(2) ability,
(3) an ardent desire for learning, and
(4) a retentive memory.

Once all the aforementioned four-angled things are attained by him, then four things will become insignificant before him:

(1) his family,
(2) his children,
(3) his wealth, and
(4) his native land.

He will then be afflicted with four things:

(1) his enemies will rejoice at his distress,
(2) his friends will reproach him,
(3) the ignorant will taunt him, and
(4) the scholars [*ʿulamā'*] will be jealous of him.

Once he exercises patience on these calamities, Allah ﷻ will honor him with four things in this world:

(1) the honor of contentment [*qānāʿa*],
(2) conviction coupled with awe and dignity,
(3) the pleasure of sacred knowledge [*ʿilm*], and
(4) eternal life.

(On top of that,) Allah ﷻ will honor him with four things in the hereafter:

(1) the honor of intercession on behalf of whomever he pleases,
(2) the shade of the throne of Allah ﷻ on the day when there will be no shade available except the shade of His throne,
(3) the privilege to provide water to whomsoever he pleases from the pool of Muhammad ﷺ [*al-Kawthar*], and
(4) close proximity with the Prophets [*anbiyā'*] in the Highest of the High Places [*aʿlā ʿilliyyīn*].

So now, my son, I have told you whatever I have heard from my teachers [*mashā'ikh*]. Now you have the choice to either pursue this field or to abstain from it."'"

These are the principles and rules Imam Bukhārī has laid out for every individual who wishes to become a ḥadīth scholar or a student of ḥadīth. We should take heed of Imam Bukhārī's advice and hold firmly onto it. In actual fact, the science of ḥadīth is even more difficult to attain than Imam Bukhārī (may Allah be pleased with him) describes.

Our present times of extreme negligence and laziness, where the maximum extent of education in this science is (normally limited to studying) the six authentic books of ḥadīth [*ṣiḥāḥ sitta*] for one to call himself a ḥadīth scholar, can be likened to "a monkey who has a bit of turmeric powder and wishes to be called a grocer." The extent to which this group of half-baked *mōlwīs* [scholars graduating from *madrasas*] has made a mock of our religion [*dīn*] cannot be found in the time of our predecessors, even if we were to search for it. The main cause for this current degeneration among the scholars stems from our confidence in our virtues and our reliance upon our defective and unsound knowledge. In fact, the jurists of the later centuries [*muta'akhkhirīn*] have prohibited us from issuing any religious verdicts [*fatāwā*] based on our own opinions. Instead, they have advised us to transcribe the verdicts from similar religious verdicts of the past. But alas! In these times, even the most intricate of scholastic issues, let alone ordinary concerns, have become subjected to the people's whims and fancies. To Allah ﷻ alone do we complain, and He alone is the Helper.

This subject is out of our present range of discussion, so I will now return to our previous discussion. In the second era, from among the numerous reasons for the differences of opinions, I have sufficed by mentioning a few reasons. During the times of the Companions [*ṣaḥāba*], Followers [*tābiʿīn*], Followers of the Followers [*atbāʿ al-tābiʿīn*], *mujtahid* Imams and the ḥadīth scholars [*muḥaddithīn*], the reasons that led to differences of opinion increased. In other words, the further we moved away from the era of Allah's Messenger ﷺ, the more the reasons for these differences also increased. This increase is quite rational because (as an Urdu expression goes) "The more the mouths, the more the statements."

Reason 5
Excessive Links Between Narrators

The fifth reason for differences is basically due to the excessive number of links in conveying the ḥadīths (between the time of the Messenger ﷺ and the current era). The more the links in conveying the ḥadīths increased, the more the disparities between them increased. The reason for this is quite clear as well. If you relay a message to someone and there are many links involved in conveying the message, an inconsistency in the message is bound to occur. This is why the ḥadīth scholars have considered a ḥadīth with a smaller number of links as having a preferential factor over other ḥadīths. If Allah ﷻ wills, I will explain this in detail at some other point. All I would say at this point is that an excessive number of links is a major cause for differences, a fact which one can determine logically, traditionally, practically and through sound discernment. According to the Ḥanafī school, the jurisprudence [*fiqh*] of Imam Abū Ḥanīfa (may Allah be pleased with him) is awarded preference over the jurisprudence and statements of the other jurists and ḥadīth scholars because, among other reasons, there are relatively fewer links between him and Allah's Messenger ﷺ. In order to clarify this, the dates of birth and death of the famous Imams are listed below:

Imam	Birth	Death	Age
Abū Ḥanīfa	80 AH	150 AH	70
Mālik	95 AH	179 AH	84
Shāfiʿī	150 AH	204 AH	54
Aḥmad ibn Ḥanbal	164 AH	241 AH	77
Bukhārī	194 AH	256 AH	62
Muslim	204 AH	261 AH	57
Abū Dāwūd	202 AH	275 AH	73
Tirmidhī	209 AH	279 AH	70
Nasā'ī	214 AH	303 AH	89
Ibn Māja	209 AH	273 AH	64

From this table, it is quite evident that since a period of two hundred years separates Allah's Messenger ﷺ from Imam Bukhārī and Imam Muslim, there are bound to be many links between them. Contrast this with the era of Imam Mālik and Imam Abū Ḥanīfa (may Allah ﷻ be pleased with them): not even a period of one hundred years separates them from Allah's Messenger ﷺ.

Among other things, an excessive number of links is one of the causes for differences between narrations. Also, since the compilation of the various ḥadīth books only began in the second century, there were relatively more narrators (at that time). This consequently brought about more differences in the wording of the narrations.

Reason 6
Weak Narrators

The sixth reason is caused by the weakness of a narration. Due to the excessive number of links in a narration, a weak or unreliable narrator sometimes finds his way into the chain of narrators. Some narrators have a tendency to narrate something very different from what they heard, either due to a weak memory or due to some other disorder. Some narrators were such that their books or their memories could be relied upon, but due to some problem or other, they began making blunders in their narrations and narrating incorrectly. This is why the Imams of ḥadīth have concluded that if a person wishes to practice upon a particular ḥadīth, he should be well aware of the conditions of its narrator. This is also one of the major reasons why the learned elders [*mashā'ikh*] prohibit the ordinary laymen from practicing upon a ḥadīth directly without the consent of the scholars. Imam Nawawī writes in his commentary on *al-Arbaʿīn:*

> The person who wishes to prove anything on the basis of any of the ḥadīths appearing in the *Sunan* collections of Imam Abū Dāwūd,

Tirmidhī, Nasā'ī, Ibn Māja, and in the *Muṣannafs* of ibn Abī Shayba or ʿAbd al-Razzāq ibn al-Humām, and other ḥadīth books which have many weak narrations, and that person has the capability to differentiate between the authentic and unauthentic, (he) is still not permitted to employ a particular ḥadīth to prove something until he verifies the continuation of the link of narrators and studies the conditions of its narrators. If he does not possess these capabilities, he is compelled to follow an Imam and he is not permitted to draw his own deductions from the ḥadīths, lest he should fall into falsehood.

At a later stage we will, Allah ﷻ willing, explain in a bit more detail that most of the jurists and ḥadīth scholars have explicitly concluded that a person cannot be permitted to practice upon a ḥadīth directly if he does not have the capacity to differentiate between the reliable and unreliable, between the ḥadīth that abrogates and the one that is abrogated, and between the general statements and the specifying statements of Allah's Messenger ﷺ. This is so obvious that it does not require any explicit mention. How can a person who is unable to distinguish between the reliable and unreliable practice upon a narration?

Reason 7
FABRICATION OF ḤADĪTHS

The era of the best of generations [*khayr al-qurūn*] (i.e. the first three generations of Muslims), gave way to the era of falsehood and fabrications, as foretold by Allah's Messenger ﷺ. (At that time,) people began fabricating ḥadīths willfully. This is why many ḥadīth scholars compiled books focusing only on fabricated ḥadīths (in order to expose them as unauthentic). Inspired by their vested interests, many of the fabricators used to concoct false ḥadīths. Consequently, whatever differences do occur in the accepted narrations will still be considered minimal (compared to what the situation could have been).

Ibn Lahīʿa says, "There was a person who was once a leader [*shaykh*] of the Khawārij (a deviated sect). He later received divine guidance to repent for all his wrongdoings. He advised, 'Before you accept a ḥadīth, make sure you study the conditions of its narrators. When we (the Khawārij) wanted to propagate something, we used to fabricate a narration accordingly.'"

Ḥammād ibn Salama (may Allah be pleased with him) narrates the statement of a Rāfiḍī (a member of the Shiite Twelver sect): "Whenever any proposals used to be passed in our gatherings, we would fabricate a ḥadīth accordingly."

Masīḥ ibn Jahm narrates the incident of an innovator [*mubtadiʿ*] who, when he repented, taking an oath, said: "We had fabricated many baseless narrations which you narrated from us, and we used to consider leading you astray to be a meritorious act."

The ḥadīth scholars have recorded many similar statements. Ḥāfiẓ ibn Ḥajar (may Allah be pleased with him) has made particular mention of such incidents in his book *Lisān*.

Some Reasons for the Fabrication of Ḥadīths

My objective in relating a few of these incidents is to point out that the fabricators themselves have confessed to concocting ḥadīths. Some of these fabricators used to fabricate solely for what they called the preservation of their ideology [*dīn*], such as the Rāfiḍīs, the Khawārij, etc. This is why the ḥadīth scholars have laid down, among other principles, the rule stating that if a person is known to have inclinations to the Rāfiḍī sect, his narrations regarding the household [*ahl al-bayt*] of Allah's Messenger ﷺ will not be accepted.

Ḥammād ibn Zayd said, "The hypocrites have fabricated fourteen thousand ḥadīths. One of them was ʿAbd al-Karīm ibn Abī al-Awjāʾ, who was hung in the time of (the ʿAbbāsī) Caliph Mahdī. While he was being hung he said, "I had fabricated four thousand ḥadīths in which I had made many unlawful things lawful and vice versa."

Some people used to fabricate ḥadīths merely to appease a king or a leader. Their stories are mentioned in detail in the books dealing with fabricated ḥadīths.

One of the categories of ḥadīth which has come under criticism by the Imams includes the ḥadīths of the Sufis and the Preachers [*wāʿiẓīn*]. The Sufis, having good thoughts of all and sundry, readily accepted all types of narrations. Considering such narrations to be authentic, they used to transmit them to others. Since the Sufis were regarded as reliable people, the others in turn accepted their narrations. Imam Muslim (may Allah be pleased with him) has dealt with this topic extensively in the introduction to his *Ṣaḥīḥ*.

Similar is the case of the "Ḥadīths of the Preachers." Many a time, preachers tended to fabricate ḥadīths merely to add a bit more spice to their lectures. In fact, some people believed that it was permissible to fabricate ḥadīths with intent to create a yearning in the hearts of the people toward the delights of the hereafter, or to instill fear in them of the catastrophes of doomsday. The narrations of the Preachers can also be found in the books dealing with fabricated ḥadīths.

Imam Aḥmad ibn Ḥanbal and Yaḥyā ibn Maʿīn (may Allah be pleased with them) once went into a certain *masjid* to offer their *ṣalāt*. After the *ṣalāt*, a preacher [*wāʿiẓ*] began narrating ḥadīths attributed to these two Imams during his lecture. At the termination of his lecture, Yaḥyā ibn Maʿīn beckoned the preacher with his hand to come over to them. Under the false impression that he was being summoned to be rewarded, he came over to them. Yaḥyā asked, "Who narrated these ḥadīths to you?" Once again, he mentioned their names. This ignorant fool did not even know who he was talking to. Since these two personalities were very famous in the world of ḥadīth, he had simply made use of their good names.

Yaḥyā said, "I am Yaḥyā ibn Maʿīn and this is Aḥmad ibn Ḥanbal. We did not narrate these ḥadīths to you nor have we ourselves heard them (from someone else)."

The preacher then asked, "So you are Yaḥyā ibn Ma'īn?" "Surely that is me," replied Yaḥyā. Upon this, he commented, "I always heard that Yaḥyā ibn Maʿīn is a stupid fool but today this hearsay has been confirmed." "How is this confirmation possible?" asked Yaḥyā. The preacher replied, "How can you be under the impression that the names 'Yaḥyā ibn Maʿīn' and 'Aḥmad ibn Ḥanbal' refer only to you two? I have heard ḥadīths from seventeen people by the names Yaḥyā ibn Maʿīn and Aḥmad ibn Ḥanbal." While this was taking place, Imam Aḥmad ibn Ḥanbal covered his face out of grief while the lecturer brushed the whole incident off as a joke and vanished.

This was one of the main reasons ʿUmar ﵁ placed constraints on lecturing during his time.

Abū Nuʿaym writes in *Al-Ḥilya* that Imam Zuhrī said, "When there are two, three, or even four links in a chain of narrators (for a ḥadīth), there is no problem with the narration. However, the moment the chain exceeds this number, it is better to remain silent."

Khabbāb ibn al-Aratt ﵁ narrates that Allah's Messenger ﷺ said, "The annihilation of the Banī Isrā'īl was also triggered by their indulging in (baseless) sermons."

Ḥāfiẓ Zayn al-Dīn al-ʿIrāqī says, "One of the predicaments of the Preachers [*wāʿiẓīn*] is their tendency to narrate anything and everything before the masses. Often, the common laypeople are unable to fathom what is being said. This eventually leads to corrupt beliefs. When this is the case with true and authentic statements, what will then be the situation with fabricated statements?"

These were the reasons which prompted the scholars to compile special books on fabricated ḥadīths. Just as they compiled books on authentic ḥadīths, they also compiled books on fabricated ḥadīths, to ensure that those who came after them do not fall into a trap of deception.

Reason 8
Tampering with Sound Narrations

This reason is also quite similar to the previous reason. Many a time, a narrator himself is trustworthy and reliable, but a malicious or antagonistic person tampers with his writings and brings about certain changes. This creates contradictions between the narrations, though the actual narrator himself is reliable. That is why his (other) narrations are not rejected: the confusion in his narration only occurred because of some other conspiracy. Those who specialize in the principles of ḥadīth study [*uṣūl al-ḥadīth*] have explicitly mentioned that Ḥammād ibn Salama's books had been tampered with by his adopted son Abū al-Awjā'. Similarly, a ḥadīth was added into the books of Muᶜammar by one of his nephews who converted to the Rāfiḍī sect. There are many other such incidents mentioned in the books of the ḥadīth scholars.

Apart from the aforementioned reasons, there are many other reasons for the differences of opinions, many of which are not worth delving into before a mainstream audience, who may not possess the full intellectual capacity needed to grasp these extremely complex issues. There is a risk that some people may develop evil thoughts of the ḥadīths due to their lack of understanding and awareness of juridical [*sharᶜī*] knowledge. Therefore, this discussion has remained brief.

The subject matter that we are dealing with is not so simple that it can be explained to all people, nor does every individual have the capacity to grasp its reality. This is why the scholars have prohibited the explanation of certain complicated issues to the laymen. Also, for this reason, our past scholars considered certain branches of knowledge mandatory even before one ventures into the field of ḥadīth. This knowledge would develop a capacity to understand the ḥadīths.

The principles of ḥadīth and jurisprudence [*uṣūl al-ḥadīth* and *uṣūl al-fiqh*] are particularly singled out as prerequisites for the field of ḥadīth. This background knowledge would enable a person to understand the reality of the ḥadīths, and he would be able to assess the truthfulness of the ḥadīths as well. Zayn al-ʿIrāqī said, "One of the shortcomings of the Preachers [*wāʿiẓīn*] is their tendency to lecture to the laymen on issues which they (the laymen) are unable to understand. This in turn leads to corrupt beliefs." ʿAbdullāh ibn Masʿūd ﷺ says, "If you narrate such ḥadīths to a group of people who are unable to understand what you are saying, it will be a cause of turmoil [*fitna*] to them." Imam Muslim (may Allah be pleased with him) has also mentioned this in the introduction to his book, and Imam Bukhārī (may Allah be pleased with him) narrates something to this effect from ʿAlī ibn abī Ṭālib ﷺ.

Weak Ḥadīths in the Later Generations

In our times, these have no longer remained very sensitive issues because the scholars of ḥadīth have already sifted through the ḥadīths. They have separated the fabricated from the authentic and distinguished the reliable from the unreliable. For example, Imam Bukhārī selected the ḥadīths compiled in his book from a collection of six hundred thousand ḥadīths. Imam Muslim selected his from a collection of three hundred thousand, and Imam Abū Dāwūd from a total of five hundred thousand ḥadīths.

Summary of the Differences in the Second Era

At this juncture, I will now terminate the discussion of the differences of opinion in the second era. The main objective of this section was to demonstrate the reasons contributing to the vast differences found in the ḥadīths. Apart from these reasons being obvious, they are also intellectually compatible. Eighteen reasons were mentioned from the first era and eight from the second era.

As time went along and the links in the chains of narrators increased, differences in the actual texts of the narrations also increased. This is one of the main reasons why there are so few weak narrations, in fact there may not be any, in Imam Bukhārī's Collection. This was so because he lived during the second century. On the other hand, many weak narrations found their way into the book compiled by Imam Dāraquṭnī because he compiled his collection of ḥadīths at a much later stage. The era of the four *mujtahid* Imams predates even the era of Imam Bukhārī. Imam Aḥmad ibn Ḥanbal was the last of the four Imams, and he preceded Imam Bukhārī. This is why there were fewer weak ḥadīths in their era, and there were not so many differences in the narrations as we have today.

In conclusion, due to the aforementioned reasons for the differences in narrations, and owing to the appearance of many weak narrations, the Imams of ḥadīth and jurisprudence [*fiqh*] realized the urgent need for sifting through all the ḥadīths. They selected all the reliable [*muʿtabar*] narrations and rejected the fabricated and unreliable ones. Thereafter, they sifted through all the reliable narrations, separating the preponderant [*rājiḥ*] from the preponderated [*marjūḥ*] and the abrogating ḥadīths [*nāsikh*] from the abrogated [*mansūkh*]. However, such sifting through the volumes of ḥadīths was obviously bound to bring in its wake differences of opinion among the Imams. Every one of them realized that certain narrators may be acceptable to one of them and not acceptable to the others, or that a narrator may be considered reliable by one of them and not by the others. This is why the Imams of jurisprudence had differences in their views, and these led to differences in their schools of thought as well, a fact which is quite natural and acceptable. On that note, we will now briefly explain the reasons which led to the differences of opinion among the Imams of jurisprudence.

Part Three

The Era of The Mujtahid Imams & Some Principles of Ḥadīth and Jurisprudence

The Main Reason for the Differences Between the Imams

As explained in the previous section, there were some changes made on the part of the narrators in reporting their ḥadīths. These changes were either intentional or unintentional, and occurred (within the narration itself) either in transmitting, or in a person's understanding of the narration. To account for this, a need was felt by the Imams of ḥadīth and jurisprudence to assess all the narrations and choose some of the narrations over the others. The Imams awarded preference to the correct and reliable narrations based on their own research. At the same time, they rendered the unreliable narrations unworthy of implementation.

It is an accepted fact that the opinions of the *mujtahids* are extracted from the teachings of Allah's Messenger ﷺ. Often, their views were extracted from the explicit texts of the *Sharīʿa.* At times, certain injunctions were deduced on the basis of a particular cause found in the speech of Allah's Messenger ﷺ.

In short, specific rules and principles are required for practicing on the ḥadīths which enable one to award preference to some ḥadīths over others. The Imams of ḥadīth and jurisprudence have differed over the matter of which principles apply in awarding this preference. It is a very lengthy discussion which we would prefer not to discuss in detail (here). In fact, the principles of ḥadīth and jurisprudence are taught even before the major ḥadīth books in our *madrasas.*

Some Principles of Ḥadīth
Types of Ḥadīths

Some of these principles will be mentioned briefly. The Imams of ḥadīth, due to the aforementioned reasons, have divided the ḥadīths into three different categories: *mutawātir* [continuously recurrent], *mashhūr* [well-known], and *khabar al-wāḥid* [a single person's report] or *āḥād* [solitary ḥadīth].

A *mutawātir* ḥadīth is one for which the narrators are so numerous in any given era that it is virtually impossible for such a large number of people to agree on a fabrication or an error. Examples of this include, the existence of Bombay and Calcutta, the number of *rakʿats* in *ṣalāt,* or the number of fasts (to be observed in Ramadan).

The second type of ḥadīth is called *mashhūr.* This category is similar to *mutawātir* in some respects, but since there is very little or no difference of opinion regarding these two types of ḥadīths, we will not discuss them in much detail here. The only difference of opinion lies in the number of narrators required for a *mutawātir* narration and whether a *mashhūr* narration should be classified in the category of *mutawātir* or *khabar al-wāḥid,* or whether it should be a separate category.

At this juncture, we only wish to discuss the third type of ḥadīth, i.e. *khabar al-wāḥid.* This category refers to those ḥadīths which do not reach the standards of *mutawātir.* Most narrations fall under this category.

First of all, this type of narration is divided into two types: accepted [*maqbūl*] and rejected [*mardūd*]. The great ḥadīth master Ibn Ḥajar al-ʿAsqalānī says, "Besides *mutawātir* ḥadīths—which are undoubtedly acceptable—all other types of ḥadīths can be divided into two categories: *maqbūl* and *mardūd. Maqbūl* is that type of ḥadīth upon which practicing is obligatory. *Mardūd* is that ḥadīth the reliability of which supersedes its unreliability. Therefore, a ḥadīth which is comprised of contradictory angles, in other words some angles pointing to its authenticity and reliability and others indicating its unreliability, will fall under the category of rejected [*mardūd*]. However, if the angles warranting its acceptability are predominant, then the ḥadīth will fall under the category of reliable [*maqbūl*]."

Thereafter, Ibn Ḥajar says that a rejected [*mardūd*] ḥadīth is not necessary to practice upon [*wājib al-ʿamal*]. However, acceptable [*maqbūl*] ḥadīths are of two types: those that are necessary to practice upon [*wājib al-ʿamal*] and those that are not necessary to practice upon [*ghayr wājib al-ʿamal*]. In other words, a ḥadīth can technically be an accepted *ḥadīth* [*maqbūl*], but due to some reason or another it is not necessary to practice upon it.

Ibn Ḥajar further states, "At times an accepted ḥadīth is not necessary to practice upon in spite of it being an accepted ḥadīth, because of its contradiction with another ḥadīth. In such a case, both ḥadīths will be compared to see if some harmony can be brought about between both. For instance, the scholars have brought about some harmony in the following two contradictory ḥadīths. The first ḥadīth states, 'There is no such thing as contagious diseases in Islam,' while another ḥadīth states, 'Flee from a leper as you would flee from a lion.' There is an apparent contradiction between these two ḥadīths, (though) both of them are authentic and reliable." The scholars have brought about some harmony between these two ḥadīths in various forms. Our aim at this juncture is not to elaborate on their opinions. All we wish to say is that where there is an apparent contradiction, the first and foremost step will be to bring about some harmony between them.

Conversely, if no harmony can be brought about between them, then we will assess whether one has precedence over the other, either in terms of its date or its occurrence. If this can be established, then the latter of the two will be accepted and practiced upon. If this is not possible, we would search for an external reason to grant preference to one over the other. However, if this proves futile, both narrations—in spite of being authentic—would be included in the category of rejected [*mardūd*] ḥadīths, because of their apparent contradiction.

The Basis of Rejection and Preference

At this juncture, two points have attracted lengthy discussions from the scholars: the basis of rejection, i.e. the causes that render a ḥadīth weak and unreliable; and the basis of preference. In other words, on what basis will one narration have preference over another in the case of two narrations that, in spite of being apparently contradictory, are both authentic?

Under these two extensive points of discussion, there have obviously been many other minor differences of opinion among the scholars. This is evident from the rules mentioned above. Let us examine the case of two apparently contradictory ḥadīths. These two ḥadīths will not necessarily be considered contradictory to every single knowledgeable person. In fact, at the very outset, the meaning of one of the two ḥadīths, according to a *mujtahid,* may not be contradictory to the other ḥadīth. However, even if there is some contradiction between the ḥadīths, it does not necessarily mean that there cannot be some harmony brought about between them. There is a possibility, according to some people, that harmony can be brought between them, though others may disagree. Once it is established that harmony cannot be brought about between them, it is obvious that differences of opinion are bound to occur regarding which of the ḥadīths should be given preference over the other. This is so because there is a possibility that one of the *mujtahids* will present such an analysis that renders one of them to be the latter category [*nāsikh*], thereby abrogating the other. On the other hand another *mujtahid* may not reach such a conclusion.

However, if it cannot be established that one is the abrogator and the other is the abrogated, then once again differences of opinion will occur as to whether one of the two narrations can be preferred over the other due to certain other reasons. We will discuss this briefly at a later stage.

Such differences of perspective among the *mujtahids* are quite natural and understandable. For instance, a narrator narrates a ḥadīth. Zayd considers the narrator to be a reliable person while ʿAmr regards the narrator to be a liar. In another case, Zayd considers this narrator to be intelligent, whereas ʿAmr regards him to be dull of perception. There could be many other reasons for these differences of opinion. In this case, the narrator's ḥadīth is acceptable according to Zayd, whereas ʿAmr dismisses him as unreliable.

In short, due to the aforementioned reasons, many differences of opinion have occurred among the Imams of ḥadīth and jurisprudence [*fiqh*] in many of the by-laws of Islam. Our objective in briefly explaining this is to expose the reasons for the differences of opinion among the scholars.

In these circumstances, one has either of two alternatives. The first is that he has the capability to assess all the reasons for the differences of opinion and he is in a position to award preference to one over the other and practice accordingly. He has the authority to do this and, Allah-willing, he will be rewarded for his efforts. Such a person is referred to as a *mujtahid.* On the other hand, if he does not have this capability to grant preference to some of those opinions over others, the next option is to follow a knowledgeable person.

Even under normal everyday circumstances, if a person does not know the road, he tends to follow someone who knows. However, before following anybody, one should examine the person he is following. Is he himself aware, or is he lost like his followers? If a person changes his leader at every cross-road, there is nothing but misguidance in store for him. This is why the scholars have compelled the masses to follow one particular scholar, and they have prohibited them from following various scholars at random.

Assessment of a Narrator

Nonetheless, due to the aforementioned reasons, the scholars have differed greatly on two different aspects of the ḥadīths.

First, they have differed on the basis of assessment [*taʿn*] of a narrator; in other words, on what grounds a ḥadīth can be considered untenable. The ḥadīth scholars have counted ten different reasons for the defectiveness of a ḥadīth. Five of these are related to a narrator's reliability [*ʿadāla*], while the other five are related to his memory [*ḥifẓ*]. The five relating to his reliability are as follows:

(1) He is a liar.

(2) He is accused of lying.

(3) He is a flagrant violator of Islamic law [*fāsiq*]. This could either be in deed (e.g. he is a fornicator) or it could be in speech (e.g. he is a backbiter).

(4) He is guilty of reprehensible innovation [*bidʿatī*].

(5) He is unknown.

As for the five relating to his memory, they are as follows:

(1) He narrates incorrectly in most cases.

(2) He has a tendency to be negligent when narrating.

(3) He has misgivings about his narration.

(4) He narrates contrary to other reliable narrators.

(5) His memory becomes impaired.

The scholars have differed on the aforementioned ten factors from two different angles. First of all, they have differed as to how these factors will render a ḥadīth weak. For example, if a narrator is guilty of reprehensible innovation [*bidʿatī*], will this render his narration unconditionally weak, or will his narration be unacceptable only when he narrates according to his innovation [*bidʿa*]?

The second angle from which the scholars have differed deals with whether or not a narrator actually possesses the defect mentioned about him. If a narrator is accused of having one of the above ten defects, does it really mean that he has that deficiency? For example, if a narrator is accused of speaking lies, this may be true according to the opinion of some people, while others may consider him to be truthful and consider the error to be that of other narrators (in the chain).

Apart from these, there are other angles of differences among the scholars. For example, according to some scholars, if a narrator removes one of the links from the chain of narrators, he is thereby considered unreliable and the ḥadīth is rendered weak. However, according to others, it is not an absolute rule that wherever a narrator is removed from the chain, the ḥadīth is weak. There is more detail to this point. The scholars will first examine who the missing link is. Is he a Companion or is he someone else? They will also examine the person who removed that link: is he reliable or unreliable? Similarly, there are many other angles from which the scholars have differed over which factors would render a ḥadīth weak. One group may consider certain points as contributing to the weakness of a ḥadīth. Hence, wherever one of those points is found in any of the ḥadīth, that ḥadīth will be considered weak and the injunction that ḥadīth mentions will not be established. On the other hand, another group of scholars may not consider these points as factors that weaken a ḥadīth. Hence, the ḥadīths that contain these points are not weak according to them, and the injunctions mentioned in those narrations will be established on the basis of those ḥadīths.

My heart desires to write more in detail on this subject, but since this is an academic topic which would bore the average layman, I have tried to be as brief as possible.

The Indispensability of the Principles of Ḥadīths

To sum up, one of the major reasons for the difference of opinion found among the *mujtahids* is that different Imams have different criteria for establishing the reliability of a ḥadīth. This is why the scholars of ḥadīth and principles of ḥadīth [*uṣūl al-ḥadīth*] consider it imperative to teach the principles of ḥadīth before teaching the actual books of ḥadīth. This enables the student to understand the reasons why some ḥadīths have been disregarded. At the same time, he will understand why scholars, in spite of an explicit proposition appearing in a ḥadīth, act contrary to it.

This is why it has always been my fervent desire to request that the people who teach the translations of the ḥadīths would at least teach a brief summary on the principles of ḥadīth. This would ensure that ordinary people, who zealously read the ḥadīths in translations because they are the speech of Allah's Messenger ﷺ, are not led astray. It would also ensure that they do not become disinclined to the juridical rulings [*masā'il fiqhiyya*], and that they do not develop any evil thoughts about the ḥadīths. All of these factors can lead to a fatal deficiency in their faith [*dīn*]. And Allah guides whom He wills to the straight path.

The author of the *Tadhkira* writes, "There is a very intricate and difficult issue in the field of ḥadīth that, since the fabricators and the preachers have fabricated many ḥadīths, and many other pious people have misunderstood the meaning of the ḥadīths, the *mujtahids* felt a need to establish a set of principles to assess the validity of a ḥadīth. This set of principles will differ from the principles set up by the Imams of ḥadīth."

There are also other factors which render a ḥadīth unreliable. Until a person has knowledge about them, it is not permissible for him to practice upon the ḥadīths directly.

Some Principles of Fiqh
PRINCIPLES OF THE JURISTS FOR THE VALIDITY OF ḤADĪTHS

The jurists [fuqahā'] have composed a set of rules for the assessment of the validity of a ḥadīth. These are placed under the heading *Bāb al-Sunna* [Chapter on the Sunna] in the books on principles of jurisprudence [*uṣūl al-fiqh*].

We will briefly explain a few principles of the Ḥanafī school (in this regard), which will enable us to recognize the necessity of understanding the ḥadīths. These principles will also expose how unaware the so-called "followers of ḥadīths" are.

The scholars of the principles (of jurisprudence) have clearly stated that just as a certain amount of knowledge is required for the understanding of the Qur'ān, there is also a need to understand the rules and principles of ḥadīth study [*uṣūl al-fiqh*]. For instance, a certain word in the Qur'ān may be common or general; it could have more than one meaning, or it could be confined to a certain meaning only. Is a certain word taken literally, or does it have a figurative meaning as well? Is a certain order given as a command, or is it optional, or is the statement giving permission to perform this action? One has to be well-versed in all these principles which deal with the significance of the Qur'ān and ḥadīth. In exactly the same way, one has to be well-versed in the principles that deal exclusively with the ḥadīths. These principles are divided into a few categories.

The first of these categories deals with the chains of narrators linking us to Allah's Messenger ﷺ. These chains render a narration *mutawātir, mashhūr* or *khabar al-wāḥid. Mutawātir* ḥadīths have already been explained [*see* page 70]. *Mashhūr* is that type of ḥadīth of which the narrators were only one or two individuals from the era of the Companions ۩, but after them the number of narrators reached the level of *mutawātir. Khabar al-wāḥid* refers to that type of ḥadīth which fails to reach the status of *mutawātir* right up to the last set of narrators.

The scholars have differed greatly as to whether the latter type of ḥadīths compels one to act upon it or not. According to the Ḥanafī school of thought, at times it is necessary to act upon them, while at other times it is not. According to the Mālikī school of thought, if a ḥadīth of this nature is illogical, it is not necessary to practice upon it. However, according to the Ḥanafī school of thought, if the narrator is perceptive and discerning (for example, the narrator is one of the Four Caliphs, ʿAbdullāh ibn Masʿūd, ʿAbdullāh ibn ʿUmar, ʿAbdullāh ibn ʿAbbās, ʿAbdullāh ibn al-Zubayr, Zayd ibn Thābit, Muʿādh ibn Jabal, ʿĀ'isha the Truthful ﷺ, and so forth), then that type of ḥadīth will compel us to practice upon it, whether it is logical or illogical. However, if the narrator is not as well-known in the field of jurisprudence [*fiqh*], his narration will not be accepted if the narration is contrary to other more rational narrations.

This is why when Abū Hurayra ﷺ said that the consumption of anything cooked over fire nullifies *wuḍū'*, ʿAbdullāh ibn ʿAbbās ﷺ dismissed his narration by asking, "If water heated over fire is used for *wuḍū'*, will it be necessary to repeat the *wuḍū'*?" Hence, ʿAbdullāh did not consider this narration worthy of establishing as an injunction.

If the narrator of any ḥadīth is unknown in the field of ḥadīth, but the other narrators who are narrating from him are reliable, then he will also be considered as a known narrator and his narration will be accepted. However, there are four conditions for the reliability of a narrator: (1) he should be a Muslim, (2) he should be sane, (3) his memory should be sound, and (4) he should not be a flagrant violator of Islamic law [*fāsiq*]. Each one of these conditions is mentioned in detail in its appropriate place. For example, that a person should not be a *fāsiq* means that he should not perpetrate major sins, nor should he be guilty of consistently perpetrating minor sins. Similarly, that a person should be of a sound memory means that he heard the ḥadīth with complete attention, he remembers it while he conveys it, and he understands the meaning of the ḥadīth while listening to it.

The second category deals with the succession [*ittiṣāl*] and interruption [*inqiṭāʿ*] of a ḥadīth. The specialists dealing with the principles of ḥadīth have divided interruption into two types: apparent [*ẓāhirī*] interruption and hidden [*bāṭinī*] interruption. Apparent interruption means that a link is missing in the chain of narrators, either among the Companions or the other narrators. The scholars have differed on this issue, as well as the issue of when a ḥadīth is worthy of establishing as an injunction and when it is not. The second form of interruption is called a hidden interruption. It is not exactly an interruption at first glance, but due to their penetrative insight and their respect to the ḥadīths, the scholars have labeled it an interruption. This is why many scholars do not include it in the category of interruption. This hidden (or rather esoteric) form of interruption can be due to many reasons. It could be because the ḥadīth is contrary to the Qur'ān. For example, there is a ḥadīth that states, "*Ṣalāt* is not permitted without *Surat al-Fātiḥa*." This ḥadīth apparently falls in contradiction to the general verse of the Qur'ān, "Read from the Qur'ān whatever is possible for you [*mā tayassara*]" (*Surat al-Muzzammil* 73:20). This is why the scholars say that the ḥadīth in question has an hidden form of interruption in it.

This form of interruption could also be due to a particular ḥadīth being contrary to a more famous authentic ḥadīth. For example, there is a ḥadīth that says, "Judgment can be passed with one witness and an oath." In other words, instead of the compulsory two witnesses required in court, if there is only one witness, an oath will be taken by the plaintiff in place of the other witness and a judgment can still be passed. However, this ḥadīth is contrary to an authentic ḥadīth which specifies, "A plaintiff is compelled to produce evidence (in the form of witnesses, etc.) and if he is unable to do so, the defendant should take an oath." On the basis of the latter narration, the first ḥadīth would not be acceptable.

Similarly, if a narrator relates only a part of a famous incident and omits the other portion, this is proof enough that the narration is a bit dubious.

In addition, if the Companions ۞ do not accept a certain ḥadīth and, following discussion among themselves, they infer their own judgments, this indicates that the ḥadīth is not acceptable. Likewise, if a narrator refutes his own narration, or he acts in contrary to his own narration, or he issues religious verdicts [*fatāwā*] against his own narration, his ḥadīth is considered dubious.

I do not wish to lengthen this subject. The specialists of the principles of ḥadīth have analyzed this matter in great detail. Whoever wishes to do so should consult their books.

THE MOST BASIC REASON FOR DIFFERENCES

In short, all the Imams—whether they are Imams of jurisprudence or ḥadīth—have a specific set of rules for assessing whether or not a ḥadīth should be practiced upon. This has contributed greatly to a difference of opinion among the Imams with regard to the ḥadīths. One ḥadīth may be accepted by some scholars because it reaches the standards set by them, while the same ḥadīth will be rejected by the others because it does not conform to their established standards. The only person who will be able to come to some decision is the one who is wholly aware of the standards and principles set out by both of these groups. As for the person who is unaware of both, he—as the Persians would say—"himself is astray, so how can he guide others?"

Quite frankly, I am surprised at the people who do not follow any particular school of thought [*ghayr muqallidīn*] who, in spite of knowing what is right, provoke the masses into believing that those who do follow a school of thought do not give much weight to a ḥadīth that is in opposition to the opinions of the Imams. The masses of those who do not follow a school of thought are, after all, ordinary laymen. I do not have any complaint against them. However, I do have a complaint against the people of knowledge who, in spite of having knowledge, conceal the truth from the masses. They are actually disguising the truth and deceiving the *Umma*.

The Four Schools of Fiqh
The Opinions of the Imams are all from the Ḥadīths

The status of the Imams is extremely exalted. It does not befit their eminence to act contrary to the ḥadīths. Not even an ordinary, unlearned Muslim would accept the opinion of a great scholar if it were contrary to the ḥadīths of Allah's Messenger ﷺ. However, it is quite obvious that when it comes to bringing about harmony between two apparently contradictory ḥadīths or awarding preference to one over the other, the opinions of the four revered Imams will take preference over the contemporary scholars. This is an accepted fact, and to refute it is tantamount to unfairness and injustice.

In short, one of the chief reasons for the differences of opinion among the Imams is the basis of preference. Some narrations may be preferred by one group of Imams while other narrations may be preferred by another group of Imams. The group that prefers a certain ḥadīth might consider another ḥadīth contrary to it as defective, baseless, or reinterpreted.

Those people who have studied books dealing with the subject of the differences of the Imams, for instance, *al-Mīzān* of ʿAllāma Shaʿrānī, *Kitāb al-Mughnī, Bidāyat al-mujtahid,* and *Kashf al-ghumma,* are quite aware of the fact that the opinions of the Imams are all extracted from the very teachings of Allah's Messenger ﷺ. The only difference lies in the deduction and inferring of rulings [*masā'il*].

We will reproduce in brief a portion of one of the chapters of Ibn Rushd's *Bidāyat al-mujtahid,* which will elucidate the fact that the opinions of the Imams are all extracted from the verses of the Qur'ān and the ḥadīths. Only the method of inferring differs.

Examples of the Multi-Faceted Methods of Inference

Ibn Rushd says, "The basis for the factors which invalidate *wuḍū'* is the verse '[…] or if any one of you comes after relieving oneself or you touched women' and the ḥadīth 'Allah does not accept the *ṣalāt* of the person who has nullified his *wuḍū'* until he performs *wuḍū'*.' On the grounds of this ḥadīth, the scholars are unanimous that the passing of urine, stool, wind, pre-coital fluid, etc., invalidate the *wuḍū'*. However, there are seven other factors upon which the scholars have differed in this issue.

First, they have differed over the impure substances that are emitted by parts of the body other than the private parts. The scholars have three different opinions on this matter.

One group of scholars considers the emission of impurity to be the cause of the breaking of the *wuḍū'*. They hold that the emission of impurity invalidates the *wuḍū',* regardless of which part of the body emits it. This is so, according to them, because the cause (for nullifying the *wuḍū',* i.e. the emission of impurity) is present. The people who hold this view are Imam Abū Ḥanīfa and his school, Imam Aḥmad ibn Ḥanbal, and Sufyān al-Thawrī (may Allah be pleased with them all). A group of Companions ﷺ was also inclined to this view, and their narrations support this view. According to this group, the emission of any impurity from any part of the body invalidates the *wuḍū',* such as bleeding of the nose, blood-letting, vomiting, etc.

Another group of scholars consider the emission of anything from the private parts as the cause of the breaking of *wuḍū'*. Hence, according to them, whatever comes out of the private parts, whether it is blood or pebbles, and no matter how it comes out, in good health or due to some illness or the other, the *wuḍū'* will be invalidated. This rule, according to them, will not apply to anything that comes out of any other part of the body. This view is held by Imam Shāfiʿī (may Allah be pleased with him) and his school.

The third group has taken into account the emitted substance as well as the place of emission. They are of the opinion that the emission of any normal substance from any of the two private parts, such as urine, pre-coital fluid [*madhy*], etc. invalidates the *wuḍū'*. However, if any abnormal substance emerges from any of the private parts, such as a worm or insect, the *wuḍū'* will still be intact. This view is held by Imam Mālik (may Allah be pleased with him) and his school.

The very same verse has been employed by all four Imams in extracting the juridical rulings [*masā'il*] on *wuḍū'*. However, since they differed over the actual cause of the breaking of the *wuḍū'*, they subsequently differed over which rules are applicable to the factors that invalidate *wuḍū'*. Due to these differences in principles, the Imams have differed in the narrations as well.

Imam Abū Ḥanīfa, Imam Aḥmad ibn Ḥanbal, and Imam Shāfiʿī (may Allah be pleased with them) maintain that even though the ḥadīth only mentions, "whatever comes out of the two private parts," this is merely a sort of prototype or example. The injunction is a general one. Hence, a woman suffering from dysfunctional uterine bleeding [*istiḥāḍa*] should also make *wuḍū'*. They also take support from the ḥadīths which mention that such a woman performs *wuḍū'*.

On the other hand, according to Imam Mālik (may Allah be pleased with him), the command in this verse is not general, but is confined to what is actually mentioned. Hence, the ḥadīths which mention a woman who suffers from dysfunctional uterine bleeding performing *wuḍū'* are reinterpreted or found to be defective by him. He considers the excess *wuḍū'* for this woman to be an unfounded practice.

The second aspect of discussion regarding the aforementioned verse on the factors which invalidate *wuḍū'* is sleep. Regarding this, there are three schools of thought among the scholars. Some of them are of the opinion that sleep unconditionally breaks the *wuḍū'*, while others assert that sleep does not nullify the *wuḍū'* under any circumstance. The third group is of the opinion that sleep will break the *wuḍū'* at certain times only, while at other times it will not affect the *wuḍū'* at all. These differences appeared among the scholars because there are conflicting narrations regarding sleep. According to some narrations, sleep does not nullify the *wuḍū'*. Ibn ʿAbbās ﵁ says that Allah's Messenger ﷺ once went to Maymūna's ﵁ house and slept so deeply that they heard him snoring. When he awoke, he performed *ṣalāt* without performing *wuḍū'*. Similarly, there is another narration that mentions certain Companions ﵃ sleeping in the *masjid*. They used to nap while waiting for *ṣalāt*, and then perform the *ṣalāt* without making *wuḍū'*. However, there are many other narrations in contrast to this. Ṣafwān ibn ʿAssāl ﵁ narrates that the Messenger of Allah ﷺ said, "It is not necessary to remove the leather socks (to make *wuḍū'*) after passing urine or stool, or after sleeping. Wiping [*masaḥ*] over them is quite sufficient. However, wiping will not suffice in a state of major impurity [*janāba*]." Similarly, Abū Hurayra ﵁ narrates, "*Wuḍū'* is obligatory upon one who lies down and sleeps."

The scholars have assumed two different stances on these narrations. Some of them have taken up the path of granting preference to one narration over the other. This group has again been divided into two; some of them have found more angles of awarding preference to the first category of ḥadīths, while the second group awards preference to the second category of ḥadīths. Finally, the third group does not find any preferential factor to favor any one of the categories over the other. Therefore, they have brought about harmony between the ḥadīths by dividing sleep into various categories. Some types of sleep will invalidate the *wuḍū'* while the others will not.

The third issue of contention between the scholars is whether the touching of a woman invalidates the *wuḍū'* or not. One group is of the opinion that if a man touches a woman without anything separating them both, his *wuḍū'* is broken. The second group asserts that this rule is not unconditional. They maintain that the *wuḍū'* is broken only if there is touching by lust, otherwise it will remain intact. According to the third group of scholars, the *wuḍū'* remains intact under all circumstances if one touches a woman. This issue has remained one of debate even among the Companions ﷺ. This is what prompted the three differing schools of thought among the Companions and Followers ﷺ. Among the Imams, Imam Shafiʿī holds the first opinion and Imam Mālik is of the second opinion, while the third opinion is held by Imam Abū Ḥanīfa (may Allah ﷻ be pleased with them all).

The very basis for the differences found among these Imams regarding this issue is that the word *lams* or "touching" (in the verse) is ambiguous; or rather, it is a homonym [*mushtarak*]. Allah says, "If you touched [*lāmastum*] a woman" (*Sūrat al-mā'ida* 5:6). The word *"lams"* has a dual meaning in the Arabic language. It refers to sexual intercourse as well as literal touching with the hand. Consequently, the Imams differed over what sort of injunction should be extracted from this verse as well. According to some of them, the verse refers to sexual intercourse. Therefore, this verse does not deal with the factors which invalidate *wuḍū'*. This is the view of Imam Abū Ḥanīfa (may Allah be pleased with him). However, according to the others, this verse is dealing with the factors which invalidate *wuḍū'*, and the word *"lams"* refers to touching a woman. Within this group, once again, there is a difference of opinion as to whether this injunction is general or restricted. According to the Shāfiʿīs, the injunction is general. Hence, by merely touching a woman, a man's *wuḍū'* is unconditionally broken.

Imam Mālik (may Allah be pleased with him) is of the opinion that this is a restricted injunction. He restricts it to lust. Only when a person touches with lust will his *wuḍū'* become invalid. Every one of these Imams has some proof or basis to substantiate his assertion. For instance, Imam Abū Ḥanīfa and Imam Mālik (may Allah be pleased with them) prove their opinions with the following narration:

> ʿĀ'isha ﷺ relates that on many occasions Allah's Messenger ﷺ used to touch her, either in *ṣalāt* or outside of *ṣalāt,* and he did not repeat his *wuḍū'* after that. On one occasion, the Messenger of Allah ﷺ was performing *tahajjud ṣalāt* in total darkness. At that time there was no lamp or any source of light in his house. ʿĀ'isha ﷺ was sleeping in front of him and whenever he wanted to go into prostration [*sajda*], the Messenger ﷺ used to move her feet away to enable him to perform *sajda* (since the room was very small).

From this it is deduced that touching a woman does not nullify the *wuḍū'*.

Now, the question arises as to whether all types of touching nullify the *wuḍū',* or only specific types of touching. According to the Mālikīs, if one touches without lust, the *wuḍū'* is not nullified. According to the Ḥanafīs, this is a general rule: the *wuḍū'* remains intact despite all types of touching. This is so because of another ḥadīth in which ʿĀ'isha ﷺ says, "At times Allah's Messenger ﷺ used to kiss his wives and, without performing *wuḍū',* he used to observe his *ṣalāt.*" Obviously, this kissing stems from lust because a person generally kisses his wife out of desire.

In short, all these differences found among the Imams stem from the differences found in the narrations, as I have explained in detail in previous chapters. This is further compounded by the various differences regarding the grounds for preference and rejection among the Imams.

Summary of the Above Discussion

To sum up, the main reason for the differences among the Imams stems from their analysis and evaluation of the various ḥadīths. At times, one ḥadīth may be regarded as authentic according to the research of one Imam, and he considers whatever to be established from it to be obligatory. However, the same narration may not reach the required stage of reliability according to another Imam. Hence, the second Imam does not consider that ḥadīth strong enough to establish an injunction based on the contents of the narration. In reality, these differences are quite in order and are completely logical.

Since the basis of the weakness or reliability of a narration is based upon the conditions of its narrators, there are bound to be differences in practicing upon the narrations as well. The metaphor for this is a sick person who seeks the treatment of various doctors. One of them might say his illness is fatal, while the other might consider it mild. The third doctor might brush it off as a psychological problem, and he will not consider it an illness at all. In exactly the same manner, a narrator might be considered unreliable and rejected by some, while others might regard him as reliable, trustworthy, and truthful. In such circumstances, neither the doctors nor the Imams of ḥadīth can be criticized. The nurse attending to the sick person or the followers of the *Sharīʿa* will be advised to adhere to whomever they feel is reliable. Allah ﷻ will assist them. Obviously, the patient who has visited various doctors cannot apply all of their treatments together. He only has to take the medication prescribed to him by the doctor he is currently seeing.

The Parable of the Imams of Ḥadīth

The Imams of ḥadīth have likened the critique of the narrators to that of a bullion dealer. The moment he sets eyes on the gold, he can ascertain whether it is genuine or artificial. Ḥāfiẓ ibn Ḥajar writes in his *Sharḥ Nukhbat al-fikr,*

> From all the various branches of the field of ḥadīth, the most complex and intricate is that of (sifting through) the defective [*muʿallal*] ḥadīths. Only one gifted by Allah ﷻ with an ingenious mind and a comprehensive memory can be proficient in this field. Together with this, he needs also to be cognizant of the status of all the narrators and extremely knowledgeable of the chain of narrators as well as the actual texts of the ḥadīths. This is why a very small group of people has ventured into this field. For example, ʿAlī ibn al-Madīnī, Imam Aḥmad ibn Ḥanbal, Imam Bukhārī, Dāraquṭnī (may Allah be pleased with them all) are some of the few ḥadīth scholars who ventured into this field.

He further writes,

> At times, the ḥadīth scholar relating the deficiency in a ḥadīth does not explicitly specify whether any injunction can be deduced from the ḥadīth or not.

Similarly, ʿAllāma Suyūṭī (may Allah be pleased with him) writes in his *Tadrīb al-rāwī,*

> The eighteenth type of ḥadīth is the defective [*muʿallal*] ḥadīth. This type of ḥadīth is the most important and intricate. Only those people who are of perfect memory and proficient in analysis are able to gain some control over this type of ḥadīth.

Ḥākim al-Naysābūrī states,

> At times, a ḥadīth is considered defective [*muʿallal*] even though there may not be any apparent factors rendering the ḥadīth as such. According to us the only proof we have for its defectiveness is memory, comprehension, and deep understanding of the ḥadīths.

Ibn Mahdī states,

> It is better for me to learn of the defectiveness [*ʿilla*] of one ḥadīth than to learn ten new ḥadīths.

ʿAllāma Nawawī states,

> The defectiveness [*ʿilla*] of a ḥadīth is a reference to a very subtle type of deficiency in a ḥadīth. There might not be any type of apparent deficiency in the ḥadīth, but there will be some inconspicuous flaw in it. This could be either due to the narrator being alone in the narration of this ḥadīth, or due to his narration being contradictory to other narrators, or due to other reasons which the knowledgeable are aware of.

Ibn Mahdī was once asked, "At times you consider some ḥadīths weak and some of them to be authentic. How do you go about determining this?" He replied, "When you take your coins to a bullion dealer, do you ask him why he considers some of them to be genuine and some to be counterfeit? In actual fact, due to excessive exposure with the ḥadīths and constant sifting through them, one builds up this proficiency."

Abū Zurʿa was once asked, "On what grounds do you consider some of the ḥadīths to be weak?" He replied, "If I tell you that any ḥadīth is defective, go and inquire from Ibn Dāra and then from Abū Hātim. If they tell you the same thing, you will understand the reality of it all." This person did accordingly and he found this to be true.

I do not wish to encompass all their opinions in this regard. My only objective is to expose the fact that the Imams have differed mainly because of the apparent contradictions found in the narrations, as explained in the above discussion. I have also explained that differences are obviously going to be found in their editing as well as their compilations.

Inference in Our Times

In our times, acquaintance with sacred knowledge [*ʿilm*] is a thing of the past. Hence, besides the ordinary layman, many deficient so-called "intellectuals" are deceptively led to believe that the inferences [*ijtihād*] of the Imams are contrary to one another (and therefore, their inferences are not reliable).

In spite of the inferences of the Imams being in contrast to one another, it does not mean that they make inference [*ijtihād*] of the Islamic by-laws according to their own whims and fancies without any proof and basis. They primarily extract all the laws from the ḥadīths of Allah's Messenger ﷺ. They only differ in their angles of inference.

In short, the main reason for the differences found among the Imams is due to the difference of the status they give to the law-bearing narrations. A narration demonstrating a certain law might be accepted by one Imam, while another ḥadīth contrary to the first one may be accepted by another Imam. The second Imam considers the second ḥadīth authentic; hence, he accepts what it says. The Imams of jurisprudence [*fiqh*] are likened to doctors and bullion dealers; it is their profession to accept or reject a narration. Hence, it would be foolish to object as to why a certain Imam has rejected a certain narration.

Today, after thirteen hundred (now fourteen hundred) years, it is not possible for us to determine whether the narrations that we have before us have exactly the same chain of narrators as the narrations of the people of the past. Nor is it possible for us to verify whether the reasons for the rejection of a certain ḥadīth which we are aware of, or which Imam Bukhārī or Imam Muslim mention, are the only reasons for the rejection of that ḥadīth, or whether there were any other reasons for its rejection.

Moreover, the status and era of the Imams precedes that of Imam Bukhārī and Imam Muslim. If this is the case with these two Imams, what about those that came after them, like Imam Abū Dāwūd, Imam Tirmidhī, Imam Nasā'ī, and Imam Ibn Māja. As for those who came even after them, like Dāraquṭnī and Bayhaqī, what status do they hold relative to the Imams? In spite of their magnificence in the field of ḥadīth, they had no option in the field of jurisprudence [*fiqh*] but to follow one of the Imams. Memorizing a ḥadīth is one thing, but to extract a juridical proposition or injunction from that ḥadīth is another matter altogether.

The second angle of differences found between the Imams of jurisprudence is due to their various reasons for the preference of a ḥadīth. Even though this was mentioned in brief in a previous chapter, I feel it is necessary to mention it separately in a bit more detail because this is one of the major reasons contributing to the differences found among the Imams.

In spite of two apparently conflicting ḥadīths being authentic, there are differences among the Imams regarding the preference of one narration over the other. In other words, what are their reasons for awarding preference to one of two conflicting narrations? This is also a very lengthy discussion. One may study the works of the four famous Imams and get an understanding of the reality of this topic. I will merely explain this briefly in the form of an example.

Sufyān ibn ʿUyayna says,

> Imam Abū Ḥanīfa and Imam Awzāʿī (may Allah be pleased with them) once met in one of the bazaars of the blessed city of Makka. Imam Awzāʿī said to Imam Abū Ḥanīfa, "Why do you—the Ḥanafis—not observe the raising of the hands [*rafʿ al-yadayn*] while proceeding toward *rukūʿ* and while rising from *rukūʿ?*" Imam Abū Ḥanīfa replied, "We do not observe this because its veracity is not established from Allah's Messenger ﷺ." Imam Awzāʿī thereupon narrated the following ḥadīth: "Zuhrī narrates from Sālim and he in turn from Ibn ʿUmar ؓ that Allah's Messenger ﷺ used to observe the raising of the hands while commencing the *ṣalāt,* while proceeding toward *rukūʿ,* and while rising from it." Imam Abū Ḥanīfa replied, "Ḥammād narrates from Ibrāhīm al-Nakhʿay and he in turn from ʿAlqama and Aswad and they narrate from Ibn Masʿūd ؓ that Allah's Messenger ﷺ would not raise his hands in *ṣalāt* except at the beginning of the *ṣalāt* while observing the opening *takbīr* [*taḥrīma*]."
>
> Upon this, Imam Awzāʿī commented, "There are only three links of narrators between me and Allah's Messenger ﷺ in the ḥadīth I have narrated, whereas there are four links in the ḥadīth you have narrated. (Hence, the shorter link of narrators renders my ḥadīth more authentic.)" Thereupon Imam Abū Ḥanīfa, comparing the two chains of narrators, said, "Hammād is a more superior jurist [*faqīh*] than Zuhrī, Ibrāhīm Nakhʿay is also superior to Sālim and ʿAlqama is also not inferior to Ibn ʿUmar ؓ in jurisprudence. If Ibn ʿUmar ؓ has the virtue of being a Companion, then ʿAlqama also has certain virtues. As for the final link in my chain of narrators—ʿAbdullāh ibn Masʿūd ؓ—there is no need to mention his virtues." Imam Awzāʿī was thereupon compelled to remain silent.

Abū Bakr Ibn al-ʿArabī (may Allah be pleased with him) writes in his commentary of *Sunan al-Tirmidhī,* "If there are any contradictions in the views of Ibn Masʿūd and Ibn ʿUmar ؓ, then the view of Ibn Masʿūd will be awarded preference."

My aim in quoting this debate between these two scholars is merely to expose the reasons of preference that each one of them held. According to Imam Awzāʿī and also according to the Shāfiʿīs, the narration with the shorter link of narrators is awarded preference over the narration with the longer chain. However, according to Imam Abū Ḥanīfa, preference is awarded to a narration according to the degree of expertise in jurisprudence among the chain of narrators.

According to the principles of the Ḥanafī school, if there is a contradiction found between two narrations, the narration of a jurist [*faqīh*] is awarded preference over the other. This sounds quite logical because the more intelligent a narrator, the more perfectly he will narrate the ḥadīth.

Similarly, according to Imam Mālik (may Allah be pleased with him), if there is a contradiction between some ḥadīths and the practice of the people of Madīna Munawwara conforms to any one of them, that ḥadīth will be awarded preference over the others. The practice of the people of Madīna Munawwara is (to him) a preferential factor. This is quite evident from his book *Al-Muwaṭṭa'*.

The Mālikī scholar Ibn al-ʿArabī writes in the commentary of *Sunan al-Tirmidhī,* "It is a principle of the Mālikī school of thought that if a ḥadīth is popular among the people of Madīna Munawwara, there is no need to analyze its chain of narrators."

There are many factors by which some ḥadīths are awarded preference over others. Hāzimī has mentioned fifty such factors in his book *Kitāb al-Nāsikh wa 'l-mansūkh.* ʿAllāma ʿIrāqī enumerated over one hundred such factors in his *Kitāb al-Nukat.*

Obviously, not all these factors are unanimously agreed upon by all of the various Imams. Those who claim to follow the ḥadīths directly are urged to analyze the ḥadīths thoroughly and determine which of the apparently conflicting ḥadīths have more preferential factors than the others. This will enable them to practice upon the ḥadīths which have more preferential factors, as opposed to those which have less.

The Approach of the Ḥanafī School of Thought

Occasionally, the Ḥanafī school of thought awards preference to those ḥadīths which have a weaker chain of narrators, or even to those ḥadīths whose chains of narration may not be as superior to the others. This is so because the narrations may possess some other more superior preferential factors. For example, the fact that a ḥadīth is in greater conformance with the text of the Qur'ān is one of the most noteworthy preferential factors that render a particular ḥadīth superior to those that contradict it, according to the Ḥanafī school. This makes a great deal of sense, because the words of many of the ḥadīths are not the actual words of Allah's Messenger ﷺ. In most cases, they are the words of the narrators who narrated the meaning of the ḥadīth, as explained previously. On the other hand, the words of the Qur'ān are the actual words (of Allah) transmitted by the narrators. Therefore, from two conflicting narrations, the narration which is in greater conformance to the text of the Qur'ān will obviously gain more preference over the other narration.

In one example of the above principle, the Ḥanafīs award preference to the narration that does not mention raising of the hands in *ṣalāt* over the narration which does mention it. This is so simply because the Holy Qur'ān declares, "And stand before Allah with ease and tranquility" (*Sūrat al-Baqara* 2:238). Hence, from among the conflicting narrations, the Ḥanafīs award preference to those ḥadīths which conform more closely to this form of tranquility.

This ruling is also established from other previous occurrences. In the early days of Islam, it was permissible to speak (and to make *salām*) in *ṣalāt,* but this was gradually abrogated and the *ṣalāt* metamorphosed into a more tranquil action. Hence, the narrations which conform more to tranquility are more juridically preferable in the Ḥanafī school.

In addition, the narrations which do not mention any recitation while performing *ṣalāt* behind the Imam are awarded preference over those narrations which mention this practice. This is so because of the Qur'ānic verse, "And when the Qur'ān is being recited, listen to it attentively and remain silent" (*Sūrat al-Aʿraf* 7:204).

Similarly, it is better to delay the Fajr and ʿAṣr prayers because it is in greater conformance with the Qur'ānic verse, "And glorify the praises of your Lord before sunrise and before sunset" (*Sūra Qāf* 50:39). "Before sunrise" and "before sunset" means a time which is close to them. A period of three to four hours before sunrise or sunset is not normally referred to as being "before" sunrise or "before" sunset. Hence, the Ḥanafīs are of the opinion that it is better to delay the Fajr and ʿAṣr prayers. Furthermore, the Ḥanafīs have chosen the *qunūṭ* (a supplication made in the *witr ṣalāt*) of "*Allāhumma innā nastaʿīnuka...*" in the *witr ṣalāt* because they were considered as two *sūrats* of the Holy Qur'ān.

There are thousand of examples of this nature, but out of fear of long-windedness, I will leave them out. All I wish to add at this point is that it is extremely important for those who claim to follow the ḥadīths directly to acquaint themselves with the elements that contribute to the weakness of a narration and to understand the factors which render a particular ḥadīth more acceptable than the others. Without this, it is not possible to practice upon the narrations.

During my student days, I commenced compiling a summary on the basic principles of the Imams and a summary on the factors that render one ḥadīth more acceptable than the others. However, time did not assist me in completing it. And Allah ﷻ is the best of guides.

Epilogue

I had written more on this subject, but I only managed to find rough manuscripts of these pages. Also, the magazine *Al-Maẓāhir* was terminated due to a lack of resources. (This was the magazine toward which the author used to contribute articles on this topic.)

My colleagues insisted that I complete this book, and it was also my desire to do so. I had lengthy and detailed discussions in mind and I had initially decided to write about four to five hundred pages, but due to my extremely busy schedule, I was unable to complete it. Since this book before you is incomplete, I had no hope whatsoever of it ever coming into print. Whenever my friends insisted I publish it, I used to put them off saying that it is incomplete.

Nonetheless, during one of my journeys to Ḥijāz, my friend Mawlānā ʿAzīz unearthed those lost pages from Allah knows where. One or two parts were still missing from the original manuscript, but in spite of this he insisted on printing it, saying that even an incomplete book of this nature would still be beneficial. My other colleagues respected Muftī Maḥmūd, Mawlānā Yūnus, Mawlānā ʿĀqil, Mawlānā Salmān, and others had also insisted that this book be published. Hence, I permitted Mawlānā Shāhid to go ahead in printing this book. May Allah ﷻ grant benefit to him as well as to those who read this book.

(Mawlānā) Muḥammad Zakariyyā
22 Jumādā ʾl-Ūlā 1391 AH

Glossary

ĀḤĀD. Solitary ḥadīth, report by a single person or by odd individuals, also termed *khabar al-wāḥid.*

ᶜALLĀMA. Great learned scholar.

ᶜĀLIM (pl. *ᶜulamā'*). Scholar, one who has been thoroughly trained and received teaching authorizations in the major Islamic sciences.

ANṢĀR. Literally, the helpers. The believers who lived in Madīna from prior to the Migration.

ᶜAṢR. Late afternoon prayer, performed after an object's shadow (minus the length of its shadow at the sun's zenith) is twice as long as the object.

ḌAᶜĪF. Weak, status of a hadīth that contains some defect—in its chain of transmission, or the proper understanding of the narrator, or its contents—or is not in perfect agreement with established Islamic beliefs and practices. It is a ḥadīth of little reliable authority.

DĪN. Literally, "a religion." Strictly speaking, it is synonymous with "Islam."

FAJR. Period of time between dawn and just before sunrise, or the *farḍ* prayer performed at that time.

FAQĪH (pl. *fuqahā'*). Jurist. One who is learned in *fiqh.*

FARḌ. Obligatory command that is established through decisive proof [*dalīl qaṭᶜī*]. One who neglects a *farḍ* injunction without any valid excuse is termed a transgressor [*fāsiq*] in Islamic *Sharīᶜa*, and one who rejects a *farḍ* injunction is considered an unbeliever [*kāfir*].

FATWĀ (pl. *fatāwā*). Formal legal ruling issued by an authorized, competent muftī or jurist.

FIQH. Islamic jurisprudence, the science of how rulings are derived from the valid sources of Islamic law, namely, the Qur'ān, the Sunna, the consensus [*ijmāʿ*] of Islamic scholars, and analogical deduction [*qiyās*].

FISQ. Properly translated as "transgression" or "deviance."

GHAYR MUQALLID (pl. *ghayr muqallidīn*). One who does not adhere to any school of thought in jurisprudence.

ḤADĪTH. Literally a piece of news, a story, or a report relating to a present or past event. In the technical sense, it refers to the reports of the words, deeds, approvals, or disapprovals of the Messenger of Allah ﷺ.

ḤĀFIẒ. Ḥadīth master, one who has memorized one hundred thousand ḥadīths by heart. Also used for one who has memorized the entire Qur'ān.

ḤANAFĪ. Follower of the Ḥanafī school of Islamic law.

ḤANBALĪ. Follower of the Ḥanbalī school of Islamic law.

ḤARĀM. Forbidden, prohibited, unlawful. The status of something that is completely not allowed under Islamic law.

IBN. Son, or "son of."

IFRĀD. Pilgrimage in which only the *ḥajj* (without *ʿumra*) is performed during the months of *ḥajj*.

IJTIHĀD. An ability of the intellectual understanding by which the subtleties, implications, finer points, mysteries, wisdom, and causes of the laws [*aḥkām*] of Islam are ascertained.

IKHTILĀF. Juristic difference of opinion.

IMAM. Derived from the Arabic word "to lead," Imam is widely used for the leader of the prayer or the leader of a school of thought in Islamic law.

ʿISHĀ. The night prayer, performed after the redness of sunset disappears.

JIHAD. Fighting in the path of Allah, literally meaning "to strive."

KHALĪFA. Caliph; the leader of the Muslim *Umma*.

Khawārij or Khārijites. The earliest sect who separated themselves from the body of the Muslims and declared war on all those who disagreed with them, stating that a major sin turns a Muslim into an unbeliever.

Maʿlūl. Defective narration.

Madhhab (pl. *madhāhib*). Juristic or theological school. For example, Mālikī Madhhab.

Madīna Munawwara. Illuminated city of the Messenger of Allah ﷺ and second holiest city of Islam (located in Arabia, today known as Saudi Arabia).

Maghrib. Evening prayer performed after sunset.

Majlis. A gathering or audience.

Makka. Holiest city of Islam which is home to the Masjid al-Ḥarām and the Kaʿba (located in Arabia, today known as Saudi Arabia).

Makrūh. Disliked. Status of something that is undesirable, and sometimes reproachable, under Islamic law but not completely prohibited [*ḥarām*]. Compare with *Ḥarām.*

Mālikī. Follower of the Mālikī school of Islamic law.

Marfūʿ. Chain of transmission that reaches to the Messenger ﷺ.

Masʾala (pl. *masāʾil*). Proposition or juridical ruling of Islamic law.

Mashāʾikh (sing. *shaykh*). Spiritual or religious leaders.

Mashhūr. Ḥadīth which is handed down by at least three reliable authorities; or according to another view, a ḥadīth which although widely disseminated later, was originally transmitted by one person in the first generation.

Mawḍūʿ. Fabricated and spurious ḥadīth attributed to the Messenger of Allah ﷺ.

Mawqūf. Chain of transmission that does not reach the Messenger ﷺ but ends at a Companion.

Mawṣūl. Unbroken chain leading to the narrating authority.

Muḥaddith. A scholar of ḥadīth.

Mujtahid (pl. *mujtahidīn*). A person well versed in the science of inference [*ijtihād*].

MUQALLID. One who adheres to a school of thought.

MURSAL. Ḥadīth narrated by a Follower [*tābiʿī*] or someone after him directly from the Messenger ﷺ without mentioning the authority in between.

MUSTAḤAB. Preferred practice.

MUSTAḤĀḌA. Woman suffering from dysfunctional uterine bleeding.

MUSNAD (pl. *musnadāt*). Ḥadīth with a continuous chain of narrators.

MUTAWĀTIR. Event or statement reported by such a vast number of people in every generation that it is impossible for it to contain any falsehood.

NAFL. Supererogatory practice.

QIBLA. Direction of the Kaʿba in Makka toward which Muslims face in prayer.

QIRĀN. Pilgrimage in which the *ʿumra* and *ḥajj* are intended to be performed together.

RĀFIḌĪS. The Twelver [*Ithnā ʿashariyya*] Shiites.

RAKʿA (pl. *rakʿāt*). Unit of prayer consisting of a standing and bowing posture and two prostrations.

ṢAḤĀBA (sing. *ṣaḥābī*). Companions of Allah's Messenger ﷺ. One who saw the Messenger of Allah ﷺ while in the state of faith (*īmān*), and then died in that state.

ṢAḤĪḤ. Rigorously authenticated ḥadīth in its text [*matn*] and transmission [*isnād*].

SAJDA (pl. *sujūd*). Prostration in prayer.

ṢALĀT. Ritual Islamic prayer involving sequences of standing, bowing, prostrating, and sitting. Not to be confused with *duʿā'*, which is simply a supplication in words that a worshipper makes without assuming different bodily positions.

SHĀFIʿĪ. Follower of the Shāfiʿī school of Islamic law.

SHARʿĪ. Legal or juridical; pertaining to the *Sharīʿa.*

SHARĪʿA. Sacred law of Islam.

SUNNA. Precedent and custom; the actions and practices of Allah's Messenger ﷺ. The second source of Islamic sacred knowledge called ḥadīth. Also used for acts of the category between *wājib* and *mustaḥab. See also* ḤADĪTH, *WĀJIB* and *MUSTAḤAB.*

TĀBIʿĪ. Follower or Successor, one who saw the Companions [*ṣaḥāba*] while in the state of faith (*īmān*), and then died in that state.

TABʿ AL-TĀBIʿĪN. Followers of the Followers. Those who saw the Followers during their lifetimes in the state of faith, and then died in that state.

TAFSĪR. Explanation, commentary, or exegesis of the Holy Qur'ān.

TAQLĪD. Following reliable authority in the affairs of Islamic law (esp. one of the four Imams). *See also MADHHAB.*

ʿULAMĀ' (sing. *ʿālim*). Islamic scholars or people well-versed with Islamic sciences.

UMMA. Community.

UṢŪL AL-FIQH. Principles or roots of jurisprudence.

UṢŪL AL-ḤADĪTH. Principles or roots of ḥadīth.

WĀʿIẒĪN. Preachers, story-tellers, or orators.

WĀJIB. Divine command established through speculative proof [*dalīl ẓannī*], though possibly strong but is of a lower category than decisive proof [*dalīl qaṭʿī*]. One who neglects or rejects a *wājib* injunction is termed a transgressor [*fāsiq*].

WUḌŪ'. Ritual ablution for prayer.

ẒUHR. Noon prayer performed just after the sun has left its zenith.

Index

About the Author

In the last century, India has undoubtedly become an important center for the study of ḥadīth, and the scholars of India have become well-known for their passion for religious knowledge. Upon them ended the era of leadership in teaching ḥadīths, codification of the special fields [*funūn*] of ḥadith, and commentary upon its texts [*mutūn*]. Such was their mastery of this science that Muḥammad Rashīd Riḍā mentions in the introduction of his book *Miftāḥ Kunūz al-Sunna,* "Were it not for the superb attention to detail in the science of ḥadīth displayed by our brothers, the scholars of India in the present era, this science would have withered away in the eastern cities. And, indeed, mastery of this science has been waning in Egypt and Syria since the tenth century AH." There is no doubt that Shaykh Muḥammad Zakariyyā was among the most distinguished ḥadīth scholars of India and a great contributor in service of the Sunna. He was given the honorary title of *Shaykh al-Ḥadīth*, or "Great Scholar of Ḥadīth," by his teacher, Shaykh Khalīl Aḥmad Sahāranpūrī, who recognized his deep insight, clear-sightedness, and extensive knowledge of ḥadīth and related sciences.

Lineage and Upbringing

He was born in the village of Kāndhlā (in Uttar Pradesh, India) on Ramadan 10, 1315 AH (February 12, 1898 CE). His full name was Muḥammad Zakariyyā ibn Muḥammad Yaḥyā ibn Muḥammad Ismāʿīl, and his lineage continues all the way back to Abū Bakr ﷺ, the great Companion of the Messenger ﷺ.

Shaykh Abū al-Ḥasan Nadwī said about him, "Shaykh Muḥammad Zakariyyā was born into a household rooted in knowledge and passion for Islam. His immediate family and his predecessors were distinguished by firm resolve, perseverance, steadfastness, and adherence to religion.... His family included many notable scholars ... and his grandmother memorized the entire Qur'ān while nursing her son [Shaykh Zakariyyā's father]."

His father, Shaykh Muḥammad Yaḥyā, was among the great scholars of India, whose primary teacher in ḥadīth was Shaykh Rashīd Aḥmad Gangōhī. Under him he studied *Ṣaḥīḥ al-Bukhārī, Jāmiʿ al-Tirmidhī,* and others of the six famous authentic books of ḥadīth [*ṣiḥāḥ sitta*]. Shaykh Yaḥyā went on to teach at Madrasa Maẓāhir ʿUlūm, in the district of Saharanpur, but did not accept any payment for his services. He instead made his living through his own book-publishing business.

As a young boy, Shaykh Zakariyyā moved with his father to the village of Gangōh, in the district of Saharanpur. Since his father and Shaykh Gangōhī had a close relationship, Shaykh Zakariyyā quickly earned the affection of his father's teacher.

Growing up in this virtuous environment, he began learning how to read with Ḥakīm ʿAbd al-Raḥmān of Muẓaffarnagar. He memorized the Qur'ān with his father and also studied books in Persian and the introductory Arabic books with his uncle Shaykh Muḥammad Ilyās (founder of the Tablīgh movement). He stayed with his father in the company of Shaykh Gangōhī until age eight, when the shaykh passed away.

At the age of twelve, Shaykh Zakariyyā traveled with his father to Maẓāhir ʿUlūm. There, under his father, he advanced his study of Arabic, tackling many classical texts on Arabic morphology, grammar, literature, and also logic. But by the time he was seventeen, ḥadīth became the main focus of his life. He studied five of the six authentic books of ḥadīth with his father, and then he studied *Ṣaḥīḥ al-Bukhārī* and *Sunan al-Tirmidhī* (for a second time) with the honorable Shaykh

Khalīl Aḥmad Sahāranpūrī. Out of his immense respect for ḥadith, Shaykh Zakariyyā was extremely particular about always studying the ḥadīth narrations with *wuḍū'*.

On Dhū 'l-Qaʿda 10, 1334 AH, when Shaykh Zakariyyā was just nineteen, his dear father passed away. This event was extremely traumatic for Shaykh Zakariyyā, as he lost not only a father but also a teacher and mentor. His deep sorrow remained with him for the rest of his life.

Teachers

Shaykh Zakariyyā was blessed to live and learn in an era considered by many to be one of great achievements in Islamic knowledge by scholars in the Indian subcontinent. He studied with few but select teachers who reached the highest levels of learning, research, authorship, and piety. In addition to his father (Shaykh Muḥammad Yaḥyā) and uncle (Shaykh Muḥammad Ilyās), he studied under the ḥadīth scholar Khalīl Aḥmad Sahāranpūrī, author of the *Badhl al-Majhūd*, a commentary on *Sunan Abī Dāwūd*. Shaykh Zakariyyā acquired a ḥadīth authorization from him and remained his student until Shaykh Khalīl's death in Madīna Munawwara in 1346 AH.

Before his death, Shaykh Khalīl Aḥmad expressed his desire to write *Badhl al-Majhūd*, and he sought Shaykh Zakariyyā's assistance as his right-hand man. This experience revealed Shaykh Zakariyyā's gift of penmanship and, furthermore, expanded his insight in the science of ḥadīth. He worked hard on the project, attained the pleasure and trust of his shaykh, and was even mentioned by name in the commentary. This indeed opened the door to Shaykh Zakariyyā's authoring many literary works and treatises over the course of his life.

Teaching Career

In Muḥarram 1335 AH he was appointed as a teacher at Madrasa Maẓāhir ʿUlūm, where he was assigned to teach books on Arabic grammar, morphology, and literature, as well as a number of primary texts of Islamic jurisprudence. In 1341 AH he was assigned to teach three sections of *Ṣaḥīḥ al-Bukhārī* upon the insistence of Shaykh Khalīl Aḥmad. He also taught *Mishkāt al-Maṣābīḥ* until 1344 AH. Shaykh Abū al-Ḥasan Nadwī said, "Although he was one of the youngest teachers at the school, he was selected to teach works generally not assigned to those of his age, nor to anyone in the early stages of his teaching career. Nevertheless, he showed that he was not only an able, but an exceptional teacher."

In 1345 AH he traveled to Madīna Munawwara, the city of Allah's Messenger ﷺ, where he resided for one year. There he taught *Sunan Abī Dāwūd* at Madrasa al-ʿUlūm al-Sharʿiyya. While in Madīna, he began working on *Awjaz al-Masālik ilā Muwaṭṭā' Imām Mālik,* a commentary on Imam Mālik's *Muwaṭṭā'.* He was twenty-nine at the time.

When he returned to India, he resumed teaching at Maẓāhir ʿUlūm. He began teaching *Sunan Abī Dāwūd, Sunan al-Nasā'ī,* the *Muwaṭṭā'* of Imam Muḥammad, and the second half of *Ṣaḥīḥ al-Bukhārī.* The school's principle taught the first half of *Ṣaḥīḥ al-Bukhārī,* and after his death, Shaykh Zakariyyā was given the honor of teaching the entire work.

In all, he taught the first half of *Ṣaḥīḥ al-Bukhārī* twenty-five times, the complete *Ṣaḥīḥ al-Bukhārī* sixteen times, and *Sunan Abī Dāwūd* thirty times. He did not just teach ḥadīth as a matter of routine; the work of ḥadīth had become his passion, and he put his heart and soul into it. Shaykh Zakariyyā taught until 1388 AH, when he was forced to give up teaching after developing eye cataracts.

Travels to the Two Holy Cities

Allah ﷻ blessed him with the opportunity to visit the two holy cities of Makka and Madīna. He performed *ḥajj* several times, and his multiple trips had a profound personal effect on him, both spiritually and educationally. He made the blessed journey with Shaykh Khalīl Aḥmad in 1338 AH and with him again in 1344. It was during the second trip that Shaykh Khalīl completed *Badhl al-Majhūd;* he died shortly thereafter and was buried in the Baqīʿ graveyard in Madīna. May Allah have mercy on him and put light in his grave.

Sincere Love for Allah & the Prophet ﷺ

Shaykh Muḥammad Zakariyyā inherited piety, honesty, and good character from his father (may Allah be pleased with him). He aspired to follow the Qur'ān and Sunna in all matters, big and small, with a passion not found in many scholars. He had extreme love for the Prophet ﷺ and the blessed city of Madīna. His students have related that whenever the death of the Messenger ﷺ was mentioned during a lecture on *Sunan Abī Dāwūd* or *Ṣaḥīḥ al-Bukhārī,* his eyes would well up with tears, his voice would choke up, and he would be overcome with crying. So evocative were his tears that his students could do nothing but weep with raised voices.

He was often tested with regard to his sincerity. He was offered many teaching jobs at two or three times the salary that was customarily given at Maẓāhir ʿUlūm, but he always graciously declined the offers. For most of his teaching career, Shaykh Zakariyyā never accepted any money for his services at Mazāhir ʿUlūm; he did the work voluntarily, seeking Allah's pleasure. Although he did accept a small salary at the beginning of his career, he later totaled up the amount and paid it back in its entirety.

Household

Shaykh Muḥammad Zakariyyā was married twice. He first married the daughter of Shaykh Ra'ūf al-Ḥasan in Kāndhlā. She passed away on Dhū 'l-Ḥijja 5 1355 AH. He then married the daughter of Shaykh Muḥammad Ilyās Kāndhlawī in 1356 AH. Allah ﷻ blessed him with five daughters and three sons from his first wife, and two daughters and one son from his second marriage.

Daily Routine

Shaykh Zakariyyā organized his time meticulously. He would rise an hour before dawn and occupy himself in *tahajjud* and recitation of Qur'ān before performing the Fajr prayer in the *masjid.* After Fajr, he would read his morning supplications and litany until sunrise. Thereafter he would go to meet with some people and drink tea (but never ate anything with it). He would then return to his quarters to read. During this time he would also research and compile his literary works, and, with few exceptions, no one was allowed to visit him at this time. When it was time for lunch he would come out and sit with his guests, who were from all walks of life; he would respect and treat them well, irrespective of who they were. After Ẓuhr prayer, he would take a siesta and then spend some time listening to his correspondence (which amounted to around forty or fifty letters daily from different places) and dictating replies. He also taught for two hours before ʿAṣr. After ʿAṣr, he would sit with a large group of people, offering them tea. After performing Maghrib, he would remain devoted in solitude to optional prayer and to supplication. He did not take an evening meal except to entertain an important guest.

Personality

Shaykh Abū 'l-Ḥasan ʿAlī Nadwī says about his characteristics, "He was extremely vibrant, never lazy; light-hearted, smiling, cheerful, friendly; and he often jested with his close friends and acquaintances. We saw in him good character and forbearance with people, as well as a rare humility; and above all, his personal qualities were always governed by his deep faith and sense of contentment."

Death

He had always hoped to meet Allah while in the city of the Messenger ﷺ; Allah granted his wish. He died there on Monday Shaʿbān 1, 1402 AH (May 24, 1982 CE) and was buried in Jannat al-Baqīʿ, in the company of the Companions and the noble family members of the

Messenger ﷺ. His funeral procession was followed by a large number of people and he was buried in the Baqīʿ graveyard next to his teacher Shaykh Khalīl Aḥmad Sahāranpūrī. May Allah forgive him, grant mercy, and elevate his status. *Āmīn.*

Scholars' Praise of Him

Many scholars, both Arab and non-Arab, have praised him and recognized his knowledge and excellence. ʿAllāma Muḥammad Yūsuf Binnōrī relates,

> Indeed there are some remnants of the scholars of past generations living today among the scholars of today's generation. They have been guided to praiseworthy efforts in multiple religious sciences, such as jurisprudence; they are on par with the previous generations in their knowledge, excellence, fear of Allah, and piety; they stir up memories of the blessed golden age of scholarship. Among these scholars is a unique figure envied for his excellence in knowledge and action, the author of outstanding, beneficial works and of beautiful, superb commentaries: Shaykh Muḥammad Zakariyyā Kāndhlawī Sahāranpūrī.

Shaykh Saʿīd Aḥmad, the head of Islamic studies at the University of Aligarh, UP, relates,

> It is evident to one who takes a look at his works that he had a brilliancy, both in knowledge and with the pen, like that of Ibn al-Jawzī and Imam Ghazālī. Of the scholars of his era, I know of no one comparable to him in this regard, except Imam ʿAbd al-Ḥayy al-Farangī Maḥallī (of Lucknow).

Shaykh Abū 'l-Ḥasan ʿAlī Nadwī relates that Shaykh ʿAlawī al-Mālikī said,

> When he reports the ruling and evidences of the Mālikī school [in his writings], we Mālikīs are astonished at the accuracy and integrity of the report.... If the author had not mentioned in the introduction of [his] book that he was a Ḥanafī, I would not have known that he was Ḥanafī, but would have definitely concluded that he was a Mālikī, since in his *Awjaz* he cites by-laws and derivatives of the Mālikī school from their books that even we have a hard time obtaining.

Students

Shaykh Zakariyyā had numerous students who spread around the world and continue, to this day, to serve Islam, particularly establishing traditional Islamic schools in India, Pakistan, Bangladesh, England, Canada, America, South Africa, Zambia, Zimbabwe, and other countries. Some of his more prominent students in the field of ḥadīth were Muḥaddith Muḥammad Yūsuf Kāndhlawī (d. 1384 AH), author of *Amānī 'l-Aḥbār Sharḥ Maʿānī 'l-Āthār,* Shaykh ʿAbd al-Jabbār Aʿẓamī, author of *Imdād al-Bārī* (Urdu commentary on *Ṣaḥīḥ al-Bukhārī*), and Muftī Maḥmūd Ḥasan Gangōhī (d. 1417 AH). Many other scholars and students also acquired authorizations in ḥadīth from him, including Dr. Muṣṭafā' al-Sibāʿī, Shaykh ʿAbd al-Fattāḥ Abū Ghudda, Dr. Muḥammad ʿAlawī al-Mālikī, and Shaykh Muḥammad Tāhā al-Barakātī.

Written Works

Shaykh Zakariyyā wrote many works both in Arabic and Urdu. A number of them treat specialized subjects intended for scholars, and the rest have been written for the general public. His works demonstrate his deep knowledge and intelligence; his ability to understand the issue at hand, research it thoroughly, and present a complete, clear and comprehensive discussion; his moderation, humility (as can be seen from the preface of this book), patience, and attention to detail. His respect and awe for the pious predecessors are evident in his works, even when he disagrees with their opinions on any particular aspect.

His first written work was a three-volume commentary of the *Alfiyya Ibn Mālik* (on Arabic grammar), which he wrote as a student when he was only thirteen. His written works amount to over one hundred. He did not withhold any rights to his works and made it publicly known that he only published his works for the sake of Allah's pleasure. Whoever wished to publish them was permitted to, on the condition that they were left unaltered and their accuracy maintained.

Hence, his books have gained overwhelming acceptance throughout the world, so much so that his work *Faḍā'il al-Qur'ān* [Virtues of the Qur'ān] has been translated into eleven languages, *Faḍā'il Ramaḍān* [Virtues of Ramadan] into twelve languages, and *Faḍā'il al-Ṣalāt* [Virtues of Prayer] into fifteen languages. He wrote four books on Qur'ān commentary [*tafsīr*] and proper recitation [*tajwīd*], forty-four books on ḥadīth and its related sciences, six books on jurisprudence [*fiqh*] and its related sciences, twenty-four historical and biographical books, four books on Islamic creed [*aqīda*], twelve books on abstinence [*zuhd*] and heart-softening accounts [*riqāq*], three books in Arabic grammar and logic, and six books on modern-day groups and movements.

Some of His Ḥadīth Works

One can find a complete list and description of his books in the various biographies written on him. Here is a brief description of a few of his more popular works on ḥadīth:

Awjaz al-Masālik ilā Muwaṭṭā' Imām Mālik: One of the most comprehensive commentaries on the *Muwaṭṭā'* of Imam Mālik in terms of the science of ḥadīth, jurisprudence, and ḥadīth explication. Shaykh Zakariyyā provides the summaries of many other commentaries in a clear, intellectual, and scholarly way, dealing with the various opinions on each issue, mentioning the differences of opinions among the various scholars, and comparing their evidences. This commentary, written in Arabic, has won great acclaim from a number of Mālikī scholars.

Lāmiᶜ al-Dirārī ᶜalā Jāmiᶜ al-Bukhārī: Written in Arabic, a collection of the unique remarks and observations on *Ṣaḥīḥ al-Bukhārī* presented by Shaykh Rashīd Aḥmad Gangōhī. These life-long acquired wisdoms were recorded by his student Shaykh Yaḥyā Kāndhlawī (Shaykh Zakariyyā's father) during their lessons. Shaykh Zakariyyā edited, arranged, and commented on his father's compilation, clarifying the text and adding a comprehensive introduction at the beginning.

Al-Abwāb wa 'l-Tarājim li 'l-Bukhārī: An explanation of the chapter headings of Imam Bukhārī's *Ṣaḥīḥ al-Bukhārī.* Assigning chapter headings in a ḥadīth collection is a science in itself, known among the scholars as *al-abwāb wa 'l-tarājim* [chapters and explanations]. In it, the compiler explains the reasons for the chapter heading and the connections between the chapter headings and the ḥadīths quoted therein. It is well known that the commentators of *Ṣaḥīḥ al-Bukhārī* have paid special attention to the titles therein, in tune with the Arabic saying: "The *fiqh* of Bukhārī is in his chapter headings" [*fiqh al-Bukhārī fi tarājimihi*]. Shaykh Zakariyyā not only quotes and compiles what has been mentioned by other scholars like Shāh Walī Allāh al-Dehlawī and Ibn Ḥajar al-ʿAsqalānī, but also correlates and clarifies these opinions and presents findings from his own research in many instances.

Juz' Ḥajjat al-Widāʿ wa ʿUmrāt al-Nabī ﷺ: A comprehensive Arabic commentary on the detailed accounts of the pilgrimage [*ḥajj*] of Allah's Messenger ﷺ. It includes the details of any juridical discussions on the various aspects of pilgrimage, giving the locations, modern-day names, and other details of the places the Messenger of Allah ﷺ passed by or stayed at.

Khaṣā'il Nabawī Sharḥ Shamā'il al-Tirmidhī: Composed in Urdu, a commentary on Imam Tirmidhī's renowned work *Al-Shamā'il al-Muḥammadiyya,* a collection of ḥadīths detailing the characteristics of the Messenger ﷺ. This commentary explains the various aspects related to the different characteristics and practices of Allah's Messenger ﷺ. It has been translated into English and is widely available.

[Adapted from the Arabic biography on Shaykh Zakariyyā Kāndhlawī by Walī 'l-Dīn Nadwī]

Also by White Thread Press

Provisions for the Seekers

Sufism & Good Character

Prayers for Forgiveness: Seeking Spiritual Enlightenment through Sincere Supplication

Fiqh al-Imam: Key Proofs in Hanafi Fiqh

White Thread Press, (first founded as Prudence Publications in the UK) is a publisher of traditional Islamic texts based in Santa Barbara, California. Its mission is to aid in the revival of the true heritage of scholarship in the Muslim Umma, and to fill the educational and spiritual needs of contemporary Muslims in the English-speaking world, by presenting, in the English language, original works by contemporary scholars and translated classical texts of scholars past. May Allah accept our endeavors and grant us guidance and success.